国家汉办/孔子学院总部
Hanban/Confucius Institute Headquarters

EASY CHINESE
易捷汉语

Understanding Chinese Ⅱ
轻松入门 下

主　　编：李孚嘉
编　　者：曹晓艳　李孚嘉　薛晶晶
　　　　　时建平　魏　捷
英文翻译：梁　泓　翟　峥
英文审订：Elyn MacInnis

U0891561

北京语言大学出版社
BEIJING LANGUAGE AND CULTURE UNIVERSITY PRESS
中央广播电视大学音像出版社
MULTIMEDIA PRESS, OPEN UNIVERSITY OF CHINA

图书在版编目（CIP）数据

易捷汉语·轻松入门：简装版．下册 / 李孚嘉主编；曹晓艳等编．
一北京：北京语言大学出版社，2010.11
ISBN 978-7-5619-2908-7

Ⅰ．①易…　Ⅱ．①李…　②曹…　Ⅲ．①汉语－对外汉语教学－教材
Ⅳ．①H195.4

中国版本图书馆CIP数据核字（2010）第216509号

易捷汉语·轻松入门（下册）

责任编辑：冯　倩
责任印制：陈　辉

出版发行：北京语言大学出版社
社　　址：北京市海淀区学院路15号　　邮政编码：100083
网　　址：www.blcup.com
电　　话：发行部　82303650 / 3591 / 3648
　　　　　编辑部　82301016
　　　　　读者服务部　82303653 / 3908
　　　　　网上订购电话　82303668
　　　　　客户服务信箱　service@blcup.net
印　　刷：北京中科印刷有限公司
经　　销：全国新华书店

版　　次：2010年11月第1版　　2010年11月第1次印刷
开　　本：850毫米×1168毫米　1/32　印张：5.75
字　　数：172千字　　印数：1-2000册
书　　号：ISBN 978-7-5619-2908-7 / H·10292
定　　价：48.00元

前 言

易捷汉语系列教材是专门为非在校学习者编写的。名为“易捷”，标示着这个系列教材的特点：实用易学，快捷速成。它的目的是让更多的人都有机会接触汉语，可以不去学校、可以没有老师、可以不用整块的时间、可以不管令人头痛的语法规则和笔画复杂的汉字，在短时间里会说一些汉语、认识一些有用的汉字，并且可以用学到的东西跟中国朋友交流或者应付一点儿实际问题。

易捷汉语系列教材包括两部：《轻松入门》适用于那些对汉语和中国文化感兴趣，想了解中国文化并想学一点儿基本交际汉语的外国朋友；《实用会话》适用于那些没有很多时间学习，但在工作或生活中又很需要用一些基本的汉语来应付工作或生活的外国朋友。

易捷汉语系列教材不仅可以做学习汉语的教材，还可以用作在中国生活、学习、工作、旅行时的应急汉语指南。

易捷汉语系列教材有图书、录音MP3、情景DVD等多种媒体互相配套，还可以通过电视网络和互联网传播，它是一个多种媒体、立体化的对外汉语教材系列，为学习者提供了多种媒体和多种学习方式的选择。

主编

Preface

Easy Chinese Series is intended for learners not studying in school. In the title of this product, the word "Easy" says it all: this is an easy and practical Chinese course helping learners to get achievement fast. It is produced in order to bring more people into contact with Chinese, and to give them an opportunity to speak Chinese, write characters, learn to communicate with Chinese people and cope with some practical problems in a short period of time without going to class, having no teachers, nor grueling schedules, nor the drudgery of learning grammatical rules and writing characters with complex strokes.

Easy Chinese Series contains two parts: *Understanding Chinese* is produced for non-Chinese who are interested in Chinese and Chinese culture, and wish to communicate with Chinese people. *Speak Out* is produced for learners who have little time, but have to use basic Chinese in their daily work or life.

Easy Chinese Series can be used not only as study material, but also as an emergency reference while living, studying, working or traveling in China.

Easy Chinese Series is a multimedia set including books, MP3s and DVDs. It can also be used via television networks or the Internet. It offers learners a multimedia, multi-faceted option for learning Chinese.

Chief Compiler

编写说明

《易捷汉语——轻松入门》是易捷汉语系列教材中的一部。它中英文两个名字的意思略有不同。中文名字“轻松”的意思是“不感到有负担，不紧张”，“入门”的意思是“得到门径，初步学会”。让广大学习者轻松地进入汉语学习，这正是我们花费时间策划和编写《轻松入门》的初衷。英文名字Understanding Chinese意在通过这部教材使学习者Understanding Chinese language, Understanding Chinese people, Understanding Chinese everything……两个名字是互相补充的，当你理解了汉语、理解了中国人、理解了中国的一切以后，自然会觉得学习汉语是一件轻轻松松、快快乐乐的事。

《易捷汉语——轻松入门》没有烦琐的语法规则和复杂的汉字笔顺笔画讲解，主要为初接触中国和汉语的朋友们阐释身在中国如何和中国人交流才能得体，如何解决文化差异；同时，在实际交际场景中展示有用的交际短语、句子，让学习者在最短的时间里，了解中国人和中国人的习惯，并得体地表达自己。

《易捷汉语——轻松入门》分上、下两册，共三十八课，每课包括以下七个部分：

- **学习主题（Subject）**：提出当课要解决的主要问题，帮助你抓住重点。

- **学习重点（Language Focus）**：分为“重点词”（Key Words and Phrases）和“重点句”（Key Sentences）两部分，为你提供解决实际交际时所需要的词语和句子。标题旁边的耳机标志表示这部分有录音。在录音MP3中，这一部分既有慢速的标准发音，为你展示清晰的汉语发音；又有正常语速的标准发音，为你展示中国人正常交际时的发音状况。

- **会话示例（Dialogues）**：为你展示重点句及其使用场景，帮助你了解中国人实际生活中在这些场合是怎么表达的。会话示例中的汉语文本、相应的拼音文本和英文翻译，分列排版，简洁又一目了然。你可以看着汉语想对应的英文是什么，看着英文想汉语怎么表达，又可以随时检验自己的表达是否正确，事实上这可以成为一个很不错的英汉—汉英练习。标题旁边的耳机标志表示这部分有录音，光盘标志表示有录像。在录音MP3中，这一部分你同样可以听到慢速和正常语速的发音；同时也可以观看DVD中的影像，看看中国人在实际生活中是怎么表达的。

- **注释（Notes）**：解释当课语言、文化中的重点难点，帮助你正确、得体地用汉语表达；在版式上，注释和会话示例左右对应，查找起来非常方便。

- **练习（Exercises）**：围绕课文中出现的句子、词语，展开不同层次的练习，帮助你巩固已经了解的学习内容。题目旁边的钥匙标志表示附有参考答案，你可以在书的末尾找到相应的答案。

- **实用一点通（Cultural Tips）**：用最简洁的语言阐述在某场景下最关键的交际文化差异，点出最需要注意又可能最容易被你忽略的状况，帮助你用最简单的汉语和交际策略顺利完成与中国人的沟通交流。

- **应变百宝囊（Language Enrichment）**：为你拓展该学习主题下的相关词语和句子。标题旁边的耳机标志表示这部分有录音，同样包括慢速和正常语速的发音。

如果你想全面掌握，当然建议你从头至尾一一学习。如果时间太紧为了应急，你也可以直接选择“学习重点”和“实用一点通”。

除此以外，书后的词语表囊括了学习主题、学习重点、会话示例、注释、练习、应变百宝囊等各个部分中出现的词语，帮助你解决在学习中遇到的障碍。

To the Learner

Understanding Chinese is one of the two textbooks of the "Easy Chinese Series". There are some differences between the Chinese and English titles of this textbook. The Chinese title is *Qingsong Rumen*. *Qingsong* means "nice and easy". *Rumen* means "to enter the gate". This title was chosen because we hope the readers of this textbook are able to take a nice and easy approach to entering the world of Chinese language study. Its English title is *Understanding Chinese*. This title was chosen because learning a language requires learners to understand more than just the language itself. When learning a language, understanding its people, culture, and society are just as important as understanding the language itself, hence the title Understanding Chinese. The English and the Chinese titles are to complement each other, for when learners truly understand the Chinese language, the people, culture and society, learning Chinese will become nice and easy.

There are no complicated grammatical explanations or teaching of strokes of characters and stroke orders in this textbook. The main purpose of this textbook is to offer beginners of the Chinese language a practical means to learn fundamental Chinese, the cultural dos and don't s, and differences between Western and Chinese cultures. In teaching fundamental Chinese, this textbook presents useful expressions and idioms for real-life situations, which will allow learners to learn practical Chinese quickly and effectively.

Understanding Chinese is divided into two parts and contains thirty-eight units, each featuring:

- **Subject** outlines the topic of the unit.

- **Language Focus** provides "key phrases and sentences" that you will need in real-life situations. The headphone signs indicate that there are recordings of the phrases and sentences in the MP3, where the phrases and sentences are read in both a slow speed and a standard speed. The slow-speed reading will allow learners to clearly hear what is being said and to focus on the proper pronunciation of each word. The standard-speed reading mimics the real-life conversation, thus making it a practical real-life learning experience.

- **Dialogues** provides a context for readers to learn key sentences and phrases, so that they can have a better understanding of how Chinese people express themselves in real-life situations. The Chinese texts, their *pinyin* and English translations are provided for easy and clear cross-referencing. In addition, the headphone and the CD signs indicate that there are corresponding recordings and kinescopes for the dialogues. Moreover, in the MP3, learners can listen to the dialogues in either slow speed or standard speed. Moreover, they can watch the video clips in the DVD that depict the real-life situations presented in the textbook.

- **Notes** provides in-depth explanations of difficult language points and cultural aspects, helping learners to express themselves correctly and appropriately in Chinese. Additional explanations are displayed next to real-life examples, making it convenient and easy to look up.

- **Exercises**, providing exercises of various levels based on the sentences and phrases occurring in the text, gives learners the opportunity to practice what they have learned. The key signs indicate that there are answer keys attached at the end of this book.

- **Cultural Tips** illustrates cultural differences in communication in some situations with concise expressions, and displays information which is the most important but easy to be ignored. This will help you communicate with Chinese successfully with the simplest Chinese and communication strategies.

- **Language Enrichment** provides you with additional useful phrases and sentences related to the subjects covered. Recordings are also available for this section.

If learners want to have a thorough understanding of what he or she has learned, we suggest that they start from the beginning of each unit and work through the entire one. If time is a problem, you may jump directly to Language Focus and Cultural Tips.

In addition, the appendix in the end of the textbook contains the vocabulary, expressions and phrases covered in the Subject, Language Focus, Dialogues, Exercises and Language Enrichment sections, which are presented in both Chinese and English for learners' convenience.

目 录

词类缩写表
Abbreviations for Parts of Speech

Abbreviation	Grammar Terms in English	Grammar Terms in Chinese
adj.	Adjective	形容词
adv.	Adverb	副词
ap.	Adjective Phrase	形容词短语
IE.	Idiomatic Epression	习惯用语
int.	Interjection	叹词
m.	Measure Word	量词
mdpt.	Modal Particle	语气助词
n.	Noun	名词
np.	Noun Phrase	名词短语
num.	Numerals	数词
opv.	Optative Verb	能愿动词
part.	Particle	助词
pn.	Proper Noun	专有名词
pre.	Prefix	词头
prep.	Preposition	介词
pron.	Pronoun	代词
qp.	Question Pronoun	疑问代词
v.	Verb	动词
vp.	Verb Phrase	动词短语

21 Lesson 21

餐桌礼仪

Cānzhuō Lǐyí

Table Manners

学习主题
Subject

A person with good table manners is considered by Chinese as polite. Since most Chinese show their hospitality and friendship by inviting you to dinner, it's important that you are well prepared for the situation.

学习重点 Language Focus

重点词 Key Words and Phrases

❶ （一）点儿	(yì) diǎnr	*m.*	a little; a bit
❷ 好的	hǎo de	*IE.*	OK; all right
❸ 好吃	hǎochī	*adj.*	delicious
❹ 好看	hǎokàn	*adj.*	good-looking; look nice

重点句 Key Sentences

❶ 多吃（一）点儿。

Duō chī (yì) diǎnr.

Please eat some more.

❷ 吃好/饱了吗？

Chīhǎo/bǎole ma?

How's everything?

❸ 很好吃。

Hěn hǎochī.

It's delicious.

会话示例 Dialogues

I

[王磊在女朋友张璐家吃饭。]

[Wáng Lěi zài nǚpéngyou Zhāng Lù jiā chī fàn.]

张璐妈：王磊，多吃点儿①啊。

Zhāng Lù mā: Wáng Lěi, duō chī diǎnr a.

王磊：好的，好的。阿姨做的菜很好吃②，也很好看。

Wáng Lěi: Hǎo de, hǎo de. Āyí zuò de cài hěn hǎochī, yě hěn hǎokàn.

张璐妈：哪里，哪里。

Zhāng Lù mā: Nǎli, nǎli.

II

[同学聚会。张华端起一杯红酒给一个同学。]

[Tóngxué jùhuì. Zhāng Huá duānqǐ yì bēi hóngjiǔ gěi yí ge tóngxué.]

张华：给你。

Zhāng Huá: Gěi nǐ.

[又给另外一个同学夹了一些甜点。]

[Yòu gěi lìngwài yí ge tóngxué jiāle yìxiē tiándiǎn.]

张华：别客气，吃啊。

Zhāng Huá: Bié kèqi, chī a.

同学：多谢啊，老同学。

Tóngxué: Duō xiè a, lǎo tóngxué.

张华：不客气，不客气。

Zhāng Huá: Bú kèqi, bú kèqi.

注释 Notes

I

[Wang Lei is having dinner at the home of Zhang Lu, his girlfriend.]

Zhang Lu'mother: Wang Lei, have some more.

Wang Lei: Thanks. These dishes are really delicious, and they look nice too.

Zhang Lu'mother: Thank you.

II

[At a party, Zhang Hua passes a glass of wine to one of his classmates.]

Zhang Hua: Here you are.

[Zhang gets some dessert for another classmate.]

Zhang Hua: Please help yourself. Eat some more.

Classmate: Thanks a lot, buddy.

Zhang Hua: You're welcome.

① Chinese often say "多吃(一)点儿" at dinner tables, which means, "Please have some more." Other expressions that use a similar pattern, you will hear when you get cold include:

多穿一点儿（衣服）。

Duō chuān yìdiǎnr (yīfu).

Put on more clothes.

And when you catch a cold, you will hear:

多喝一点儿水。

Duō hē yìdiǎnr shuǐ.

Drink some more water.

② [好吃] means "delicious" or "taste good". Similar expressions that combine "好" and one of the senses are:

好＋喝(hē) → 好喝 taste good

好＋听(tīng) → 好听 sound good

好＋看(kàn) → 好看 look good

好＋闻(wén) → 好闻 smell good

会话示例 Dialogues

Ⅲ

[李洋请客户吃饭。]

李洋：你们吃好了③吗？

客户：好了，谢谢！

[Lǐ Yáng qǐng kèhù chī fàn.]

Lǐ Yáng: Nǐmen chīhǎole ma?

Kèhù: Hǎo le, xièxie!

Ⅳ

[几个朋友在饭店吃完饭。]

A：服务员，买单④！

……

B：打电话之前说好的。这次我请，下次你请！

……

C：你们俩别争了。我已经结完了。

[Jǐ ge péngyou zài fàndiàn chīwán fàn.]

A: Fúwùyuán, mǎidān!

……

B: Dǎ diànhuà zhī qián shuōhǎo de. zhèi cì wǒ qǐng, xià cì nǐ qǐng!

……

C: Nǐmen liǎ bié zhēng le. wǒ yǐjīng jiéwán le.

注释 Notes

III

[*Li Yang takes some clients out to dinner.*]

Li Yang: How's everything?

Clients: Great ! Thanks a lot.

IV

[*A group of people have just finished their meal in a restaurant.*]

A: Waiter, check please.

...

B: I thought we had a deal. It's my treat this time and your turn next time.

...

C: No need to argue. I've paid the bill already.

③ [吃饱] and[吃好] both follow the pattern of a verb plus a supplement. Similar phrases are "吃完chīwán (finish one's meal)" and "买到mǎidào (have bought something)". "饱" or "好" indicates the result of an action, or the status of that result. Toward the end of the dinner, the host/hostess always asks the guests if they are satisfied with the meal to show his/her hospitality. "吃好了吗？" is more polite and used on more formal occasions, whereas "吃饱了吗？" is often used between friends and acquaintances.

④ You can say "结账" or "买单" at the end of a meal to ask the waiter to bring you the check.

练习 Exercises

一、根据英文提示，将下面的词语连接成一句话。

Make sentences with the given words and phrases.

1. Please eat some more.

____

多 一点儿 请 吃

duō yìdiǎnr qǐng chī

2. This dish is very delicious.

____

这 菜 很 好吃

zhè cài hěn hǎochī

二、意念表达。

Express the following functions and notions.

1. A friend invites you to dinner. Tell him/her how much you like the dishes.
2. Ask for the check at the end of the dinner.

三、根据语境，完成会话。

Complete the dialogues according to the context.

1. A：你吃好了吗？
   Nǐ chīhǎole ma?
   How's everything?

   B：____________________

2. A：不要客气，多吃点儿。
   Búyào kèqi, duō chī diǎnr.
   Please help yourself. Have some more.

   B：____________________

四、实践汉语。

Practice your Chinese.

Invite your friends, old and new, Chinese and otherwise, to have a potluck dinner at your place.

实用一点通
Cultural Tips

In general, although the food is put in a big dish at the center of the table for all to take from, it's a good manner to take your portion in one move and please don't move your chopsticks to and fro inside the big plate if you don't want to leave a bad impression to others. If you're not skillful at chopsticks and not sure about taking your portion to your own plate in one move, use "public" chopsticks or spoon instead. Moreover, if you invite others to dinner, then you can take food for those sitting next to you to show your hospitality and sincerity.

应变百宝囊
Language Enrichment

1	口水鸡	Kǒushuǐ Jī	Spicy Sichuan chicken
2	古老肉	Gūlǎo Ròu	Sweet and sour pork
3	回锅肉	Huíguō Ròu	Twice cooked pork
4	辣子鸡丁	Làzi Jīdīng	Diced chicken with chili
5	麻婆豆腐	Mápó Dòufu	Bean curd cooked in hot sauce
6	拔丝苹果	Básī Píngguǒ	Apple in hot toffee
7	京酱肉丝	Jīngjiàng Ròusī	Sweet shredded pork with Chinese onions
8	北京烤鸭	Běijīng Kǎoyā	Peking roast duck

22 Lesson 22

表达需要

Biǎodá Xūyào

Expressing Wants & Intentions

学习主题 Subject

Here you will learn useful expressions to get you a drink. Even if you forget these expressions, you can still get what you want. And here's how.

学习重点 Language Focus

重点词 Key Words and Phrases

1	喝	hē	*v.*	drink
2	牛奶	niúnǎi	*n.*	milk
3	可乐	kělè	*n.*	coke
4	冰	bīng	*n.*	ice
5	水	shuǐ	*n.*	water
6	茶	chá	*n.*	tea
7	红茶	hóngchá	*n.*	black tea
8	绿茶	lǜchá	*n.*	green tea
9	花茶	huāchá	*n.*	scented tea
10	乌龙茶	wūlóngchá	*n.*	oolong tea

重点句 Key Sentences

1. 我想喝茶。
   Wǒ xiǎng hē chá.
   I want some tea.

2. 我要一壶绿茶。
   Wǒ yào yì hú lǜchá.
   I want a pot of green tea.

3. 有牛奶吗?
   Yǒu niúnǎi ma?
   Do you have milk?

4. 你们想喝点儿什么?
   Nǐmen xiǎng hē diǎnr shénme?
   What do you want to drink?

5. 给我来一瓶可乐。
   Gěi wǒ lái yì píng kělè.
   I want a coke.

6. 你喝红茶、绿茶，还是花茶?
   Nǐ hē hóngchá、lǜchá, háishi huāchá?
   What would you like, black tea, green tea, or scented tea?

会话示例 Dialogues

I

[咖啡馆里。]

服务员：你们想喝点儿什么？

顾客A：有牛奶吗？

服务员：有。

顾客A：我要一杯牛奶。

顾客B：有可乐吗？

服务员：有。

顾客B：给我来①一瓶可乐。

[Kāfēiguǎn li.]

Fúwùyuán: Nǐmen xiǎng hē diǎnr shénme?

Gùkè A: Yǒu niúnǎi ma?

Fúwùyuán: Yǒu.

Gùkè A: Wǒ yào yì bēi niúnǎi.

Gùkè B: Yǒu kělè ma?

Fúwùyuán: Yǒu.

Gùkè B: Gěi wǒ lái yì píng kělè.

II

[茶馆里。]

服务员：你们想喝点儿什么？

顾客A：小姐，有冰水②吗？

服务员：有。

顾客A：我要③一杯冰水。

顾客B：我要喝茶。

服务员：你喝红茶、绿茶还是④花茶？

顾客B：我要一壶绿茶。

[Cháguǎn li.]

Fúwùyuán: Nǐmen xiǎng hē diǎnr shénme?

Gùkè A: Xiǎojiě, yǒu bīng shuǐ ma?

Fúwùyuán: Yǒu.

Gùkè A: Wǒ yào yì bēi bīng shuǐ.

Gùkè B: Wǒ yào hē chá.

Fúwùyuán: Nǐ hē hóngchá、lǜchá háishi huāchá?

Gùkè B: Wǒ yào yì hú lǜchá.

注释 Notes

I

[*At a café.*]

Waitress: What do you want to drink?

Customer A: Do you have milk?

Waitress: Yes.

Customer A: I'd like a glass of milk, then.

Customer B: Do you have coke?

Waitress: Sure.

Customer B: A bottle of coke, please.

II

[*At a tea house.*]

Waitress: What would you like?

Customer A: Do you have ice water?

Waitress: Yes, we do.

Customer A: A glass of ice water, please.

Customer B: I want some tea.

Waitress: Black tea, green tea, or scented tea?

Customer B: I'd like a pot of green tea.

① [来]is one of the frequently-used words in Chinese, and its meaning depends on the context. For instance, "来一个水煮鱼" (We'll have/order a boiled fish in spicy soup)". Here, "来" means "have" or "order". Sometimes, at a dinner table, when your host/hostess keeps helping you with food, you can say "我自己来吧", which means "I'll help myself ", but most probably your host/hostess will still keep helping you. Just take it easy and enjoy his / her hospitality.

② Chinese often drink hot water, and most restaurants do not serve ice water, but you can ask the waiter/waitress if you want ice water or other iced drinks.

③ [想]and[要]can both be followed by a verb to express a plan or wish to do something. "要", which is similar to "want", is stronger than "想", which is similar to "would like to". If you don't want to do something, you can use "不想", which is less strong and therefore sounds more polite. For instance, in the dialogue, the waitress asks, "你们想喝些什么？(What would you like to drink ?)" Another difference between "要" and "想" is that "要" can be followed by nouns while "想" cannot. You can say, for instance, "我要一杯冰水。(I want a glass of ice water.)"

会话示例 Dialogues

Ⅲ

[小张和一位外国朋友在聊天喝茶。]

朋友：这个茶味道真好，这是什么茶？

小张：铁观音，是乌龙茶⑤。

[Xiǎo Zhāng hé yí wèi wàiguó péngyou zài liáo tiān hē chá.]

Péngyou: Zhège chá wèidào zhēn hǎo, zhè shì shénme chá?

Xiǎo Zhāng: Tiěguānyīn, shì wūlóngchá.

注释 Notes

III

[Xiao Zhang is drinking tea and chatting with a foreign friend.]

Friend: It tastes really good. What kind of tea is it?

Xiao Zhang: It's called Tieguanyin, a type of oolong tea.

④ [还是] is used in an alternative question, and is placed before the last alternative.

⑤ China boasts a great variety of tea. Based on the degree of fermentation, tea is divided into green tea (Longjing of Hangzhou and Biluochun of Taihu Lake), black tea (Qihong of Anhui Province and Dianhong of Yunnan Province), scented tea (jasmine tea), and oolong tea (Tieguanyin).

练习 Exercises

一、从右栏给左栏的词语找到相应的英文释义，并组织句子。

Match the Chinese expressions with the English ones, and make sentences with them.

想	xiǎng	a bit
喝	hē	drink
你	nǐ	what
（一）点儿	(yì) diǎnr	you
什么	shénme	want

The sentence you make is:

____

一	yī	I
我	wǒ	green tea
壶	hú	pot
要	yào	one
绿茶	lǜchá	want

The sentence you make is:

____

二、意念表达。

Express the following functions and notions.

1. You're thirsty and want some drink.
2. You have a variety of tea and ask your guests what they prefer.

三、根据提示，完成对话。

Make dialogues with the given words.

You are at a tea house with some friends to experience the tea culture of China. Complete the dialogues.

You: 你想喝点儿什么?

Nǐ xiǎng hē diǎnr shénme?

What would you like to drink?

Friend: 这儿________咖啡吗?（有yǒu、还有hái yǒu、没有méiyǒu）

Zhèr________kāfēi ma?

Do they have coffee?

You: 这是茶馆，有红茶、花茶，________绿茶，没有咖啡。（有yǒu、还有hái yǒu、没有méiyǒu）

Zhè shì cháguǎn, yǒu hóngchá、huāchá, ________ lǜchá, méiyǒu kāfēi.

This is a tea house. I think they have black tea, scented tea, green tea, but I'm afraid they don't sell coffee.

Friend: 那我________绿茶。（想xiǎng、要yào、有yǒu）

Nà wǒ ________ lǜchá.

Then, I'll have some green tea.

You: 我也喜欢绿茶。

Wǒ yě xǐhuan lǜchá.

I like green tea too.

You (to waitress): 小姐，________（想xiǎng、来lái、喝hē）一________（个gè、杯bēi、壶hú）绿茶。

Xiǎojiě, ________ yì ________ lǜchá.

A pot of green tea for us, please.

四、实践汉语。

Practice your Chinese.

Those pictures with a check show what you'd like to order. Tell the waiter / waitress the drink you want using the words giving.

1. 杯bēi cup；绿茶lǜchá green tea；红茶hóngchá black tea

(✓)

(×)

2. 杯bēi cup/glass；咖啡kāfēi coffee；可乐kělè coke

(✓)

(×)

3. 瓶píng bottle；杯bēi cup；可乐kělè coke；花茶huāchá scented tea

(✓)

(×)

实用一点通
Cultural Tips

Most Chinese favor tea leaves instead of tea bags or powdered tea. Generally, they would have tea alone, without adding either sugar or milk, for they love the taste of tea in water. If you have tea in a Chinese tea house or restaurant, don't blame waiter/waitress for not bring you sugar and milk. Next time when you go to have tea at a tea house, pay attention to the tea sets, tea leaves, the performance of the waiter / waitress there, and you'll enjoy your time more.

应变百宝囊
Language Enrichment

❶ 果汁	guǒzhī	juice
❷ 矿泉水	kuàngquánshuǐ	mineral water
❸ 橙汁	chéngzhī	orange juice
❹ 白酒	báijiǔ	liquor
❺ 红酒	hóngjiǔ	red wine
❻ 汽水	qìshuǐ	soda
❼ 啤酒	píjiǔ	beer

23 Lesson 23

时间 I（时点）

Shíjiān I (Shídiǎn)

Expressing Time

学习主题 Subject

To enquire about and to specify time are important, especially when you take a train or flight, see a movie or have an appointment. Here you will learn how to express time and how to confirm a date in Chinese.

学习重点 Language Focus

重点词 Key Words and Phrases

❶ 几	jǐ	*qp.*	how many
❷ 点	diǎn	*n.*	o'clock
❸ 刻	kè	*n.*	quarter
❹ 分	fēn	*n.*	minute
❺ 半	bàn	*num.*	half

重点句 Key Sentences

❶ 劳驾，几点了？

Láo jià, jǐ diǎn le?

Excuse me, what time is it?

❷ 八点零八分。

Bā diǎn líng bā fēn.

Eight past eight.

❸ 四点一刻。

Sì diǎn yí kè.

A quarter past four.

❹ 两点半。

Liǎng diǎn bàn.

Two thirty.

❺ 晚上见。

Wǎnshang jiàn.

See you in the evening.

会话示例 Dialogues

I

[马路上，一位行人询问时间。]

A: 劳驾①!

B: 你好!

A: 请问几点了②?

B: 四点一刻了。

A: 谢谢。

[Mǎlù shang, yí wèi xíngrén xúnwèn shíjiān.]

A: Láo jià!

B: Nǐ hǎo!

A: Qǐngwèn jǐ diǎn le?

B: Sì diǎn yí kè le.

A: Xièxie.

II

[办公室里，两位同事聊天。]

A: 晚上去看电影吧。

B: 好啊，几点的?

A: 七点四十五分③的。

B: 在哪儿见面?

A: 在电影院门口吧，七点，我在那儿等你。

B: 好，那咱们晚上见。

A: 晚上见。

[Bàngōngshì li, liǎng wèi tóngshì liáo tiān.]

A: Wǎnshang qù kàn diànyǐng ba.

B: Hǎo a, jǐ diǎn de?

A: Qī diǎn sìshíwǔ fēn de.

B: Zài nǎr jiàn miàn?

A: Zài diànyǐngyuàn ménkǒu ba, qī diǎn, wǒ zài nàr děng nǐ.

B: Hǎo, nà zánmen wǎnshang jiàn.

A: Wǎnshang jiàn.

注释 Notes

I

[*A person is asking about the time in the street.*]

A: Excuse me!

B: Yes?

A: What time is it?

B: A quarter past four.

A: Thanks.

II

[*Two colleagues are discussing what to do after work in the office.*]

A: Let's go to a movie tonight.

B: Good idea. What time does it start?

A: Seven forty-five.

B: Where shall we meet?

A: How about seven in front of the cinema?

B: Sure. See you in the evening.

A: See you then.

① [劳驾] means "Excuse me/ Would you please.../May I trouble you to...". When you are asking someone to help you or step aside so that you can walk through, you may start by saying "劳驾" followed by your request.

② [几] is often used to refer to a number less than 10 except when referring to time. You are supposed to use "几" to ask about any specific time. Even if it's later than ten o'clock, for instance, "十一点(eleven o'clock)", or "十二点(twelve o'clock)", you still need to use "几点了？" if you want to know what time it is. The same applies to month and date.

③ How to read time : there is no big difference in denoting time between Chinese and English, except in the case of 2 which reads "liǎng" instead of "èr", for instance,

2:00 (two o'clock)
两点 liǎng diǎn
2:05 (five past two)
两点零五（分）liǎng diǎn líng wǔ (fēn)
两点过五分 liǎng diǎn guò wǔ fēn

会话示例 Dialogues

Ⅲ

[火车站前。]

A：请问，从上海来的22次[4]几点到？

B：八点零八分。

A：谢谢。

B：不客气。

[Huǒchēzhàn qián.]

A: Qǐngwèn, cóng Shànghǎi lái de èrshí'èr cì jǐ diǎn dào?

B: Bā diǎn líng bā fēn.

A: Xièxie.

B: Bú kèqi.

注释 Notes

III

[*At a railway station.*]

A: Excuse me, when does No. 22 train from Shanghai pull in?

B: At eight eight.

A: Thank you.

B: You're welcome.

2:15 (a quarter past two, two fifteen)
两点十五（分）liǎng diǎn shíwǔ (fēn)
两点一刻 liǎng diǎn yí kè
2:30 (half past two, two thirty)
两点三十（分）liǎng diǎn sānshí (fēn)
两点半 liǎng diǎn bàn
2:45 (a quarter to three, two forty-five)
两点四十五（分）liǎng diǎn sìshíwǔ (fēn)
两点三刻 liǎng diǎn sān kè
差一刻三点 chà yí kè sān diǎn

④ [次] refers to train number. In China, train is numbered by "number+次". Usually, trains departing from Beijing are odd-numbered, whereas those heading for Beijing are even-numbered, Based on their speed, trains are divided into the following categories:

Common express train 1483次
Express train K180次
Special express train T5 次
Through express train Z21次
China Railway High-speed train D31次
China High-speed train G1022次

练习
Exercises

一、根据英文提示，用汉语说出下面的句子。
Translate the following sentences into Chinese.

1. What time is it?

____

2. I will meet you at eight ten.

____

二、根据图示，用汉语回答问题。
Answer the questions according to the pictures.

1. A：劳驾，几点了？

Láo jià, jǐ diǎn le?

Excuse me, what time is it?

B：________________（刻 kè quarter）

2. A：请问，T8次列车几点到？

Qǐngwèn, T8 cì lièchē jǐ diǎn dào?

Excuse me, when does the T8 train arrive?

B：________________（半 bàn half）

三、看例句，组成对话。
Complete the dialogues following the example.

例：我喜欢宫保鸡丁。

Wǒ xǐhuan Gōngbǎo Jīdīng.

I like Kung Pao Chicken.

Q：他喜欢<u>什么</u>？

Tā xǐhuan <u>shénme</u>?

What does he like?

A：他喜欢宫保鸡丁。

Tā xǐhuan Gōngbǎo Jīdīng.

He likes Kung Pao Chicken.

1. 我<u>八点</u>去北京饭店。

Wǒ bā diǎn qù Běijīng Fàndiàn.

I'm going to Beijing Hotel at eight.

Q：他______去北京饭店？

Tā______qù Běijīng Fàndiàn?

When is he going to Beijing Hotel ?

A：他八点去北京饭店。

Tā bā diǎn qù Běijīng fàndiàn.

He's going there at eight.

2. 我们晚上去看<u>电影</u>吧。

Wǒmen wǎnshang qù kàn diànyǐng ba.

Let's go to a movie this evening.

Q：他们晚上去看______？

Tāmen wǎnshang qù kàn ______?

What are they going to see this evening?

A：他们晚上去看电影。

Tāmen wǎnshang qù kàn diànyǐng.

They are going to see a movie.

3. 我在<u>电影院门口</u>等你。

Wǒ zài diànyǐngyuàn ménkǒu děng nǐ.

I'll see you in front of the cinema.

Q：他在______等你？

Tā zài______děng nǐ?

Where will he be waiting for you?

A：他在电影院门口等我。

Tā zài diànyǐngyuàn ménkǒu děng wǒ.

He'll be waiting for me in front of the cinema.

四、实践汉语。

Practice your Chinese.

Your mother calls you and asks how you're going to spend the weekend. Tell her your plan.

实用一点通 Cultural Tips

China has a vast territory and spans four times zones, but the entire country adopts universally the "Beijing Time", a standard time of Beijing and the 8th Time Zone East. Therefore, when you ask about time all over the country, people will give you the same answer. The local radio stations and call service will also give you the "Beijing Time".

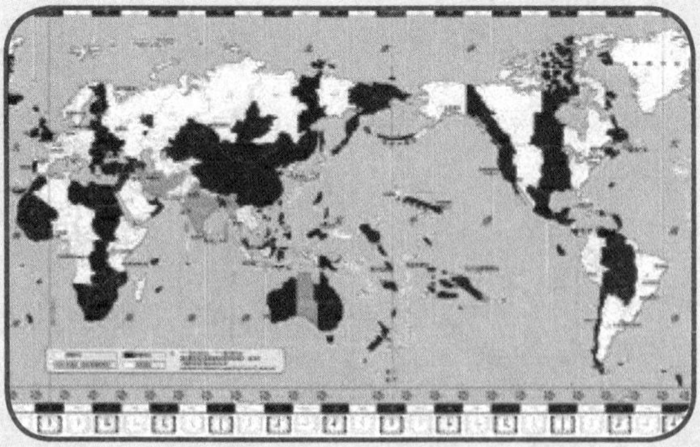

应变百宝囊
Language Enrichment

❶	公共汽车	gōnggòng qìchē	bus
❷	汽车站	qìchēzhàn	bus stop
❸	地铁	dìtiě	subway
❹	过街天桥	guòjiē tiānqiáo	overpass
❺	火车	huǒchē	train
❻	火车站	huǒchēzhàn	railway station
❼	飞机	fēijī	airplane
❽	飞机场	fēijīchǎng	airport
❾	轮船	lúnchuán	ship
❿	码头	mǎtou	dock

24 Lesson 24

时间 II（时段）

Shíjiān II (Shíduàn)

Expressing Duration

学习主题 Subject

You have learned how to express a specific time, but there're also situations requiring you to specify a period of time. For example, when you go to see a doctor and are asked the question of when your fever started, you won't give him/her an exact time. Here you will learn what a Chinese will say in such a situation.

学习重点 Language Focus

重点词 Key Words and Phrases

❶	什么	shénme	*qp.*	what
❷	时候	shíhou	*n.*	(a point in) time
❸	什么时候	shénme shíhou	*IE.*	when
❹	早上	zǎoshang	*n.*	morning
❺	上午	shàngwǔ	*n.*	morning
❻	中午	zhōngwǔ	*n.*	noon
❼	下午	xiàwǔ	*n.*	afternoon
❽	晚上	wǎnshang	*n.*	evening, night

重点句 Key Sentences

❶ 下午四点半下班。

Xiàwǔ sì diǎn bàn xià bān.

I get off work at four thirty every afternoon.

❷ 什么时候开始的？

Shénme shíhou kāishǐ de?

When did it start?

会话示例 Dialogues

I

[医院里。]

护士：你怎么了？

病人：我发烧。

护士：什么时候①开始的？

病人：今天早上②开始的。

[Yīyuàn li.]

Hùshi: Nǐ zěnme le?

Bìngrén: Wǒ fāshāo.

Hùshi: Shénme shíhou kāishǐ de?

Bìngrén: Jīntiān zǎoshang kāishǐ de.

II

[我的一天]

我早上6点起床。我们早上8点半③上班。我7点半从家走。上午我常常在办公室处理文件。我们中午12点吃午饭。下午1点开始工作。下午我常常开会，或者接待客户，很忙。我们下午4点半下班。晚上我7点吃晚饭。晚上我喜欢看看电视，然后看看书、听听音乐。晚上我11点睡觉 。

[Wǒ de yì tiān]

Wǒ zǎoshang liù diǎn qǐ chuáng. Wǒmen zǎoshang bā diǎn bàn shàng bān. Wǒ qī diǎn bàn cóng jiā zǒu. Shàngwǔ wǒ chángcháng zài bàngōngshì chǔlǐ wénjiàn. Wǒmen zhōngwǔ shí'èr diǎn chī wǔfàn. Xiàwǔ yī diǎn kāishǐ gōngzuò. Xiàwǔ wǒ chángcháng kāi huì, huòzhě jiēdài kèhù, hěn máng. Wǒmen xiàwǔ sì diǎn bàn xià bān. Wǎnshang wǒ qī diǎn chī wǎnfàn. Wǎnshang wǒ xǐhuan kànkan diànshì, ránhòu kànkan shū、tīngting yīnyuè. Wǎnshang wǒ shíyī diǎn shuìjiào.

注释 Notes

I

[*In a hospital.*]

Nurse: Can I help you?

Patient: I'm having a fever.

Nurse: When did it start?

Patient: Only this morning.

II

[*My Typical Day*]

I usually get up at six. We start to work at half past eight, and I leave home at seven thirty. In the morning, I often deal with some paper work in the office. Then, we have lunch at noon, and start the work from one o'clock. I often go to meetings or meet clients. After a busy day, we get off work at half past four. I usually have supper at seven and after that, I watch TV, read, or listen to music until about eleven when I go to bed.

① [什么时候] is equivalent to "when", with "什么 (what)" and "时候 (moment, time)". The two words must be used together to indicate "when".

② In Chinese, When expressing time, a larger unit goes before the smaller one, which is just the opposite of the English tradition. This is because of Chinese way of thinking.

③ You must also note that when you are to indicate the time of a certain action or an event, the time word must precede the verb or the verbal structure, such as "中午12点吃午饭 (I usually have lunch at twelve.)" in the case of "My Typical Day". In addition, time word can also be placed at the beginning of a sentence, such as "我7点吃晚饭(I have supper at seven.)" and "晚上我喜欢看看电视 (I like watching TV in the evening.)", etc.

练习 Exercises

一、从右栏给左栏的词语找以相应的英文释义，并组织句子。

Match the Chinese words with the English ones, and make sentences.

你	nǐ	not, no
不	bù	what
时候	shíhou	you
舒服	shūfu	comfortable
开始	kāishǐ	begin
什么	shénme	(a point in)time

The sentence you make is:

____

八	bā	eight
我	wǒ	go to work
早上	zǎoshang	o'clock
点	diǎn	morning
半	bàn	I, me
上班	shàng bān	half

The sentence you make is:

____

二、根据实际情况，用汉语回答问题。

Answer the questions in Chinese according to your situation.

1. Q：你早上几点起床？
   Nǐ zǎoshang jǐ diǎn qǐ chuáng?
   When do you get up?
   A：________________

2. Q：晚上你常常做什么？
   Wǎnshang nǐ chángcháng zuò shénme?
   What do you usually do in the evening?
   A：________________

三、根据语境，完成对话。

Complete the dialogues according to the context.

1. A：______________________?

   B：上午我常常处理文件。

   Shàngwǔ wǒ chángcháng chǔlǐ wénjiàn.

   I usually deal with some paper work in the morning.

2. A：______________________?

   B：星期六我睡觉、听音乐、看电影。

   Xīngqīliù wǒ shuìjiào、tīng yīnyuè、kàn diànyǐng.

   I often sleep, listen to music or go to a movie on Saturdays.

3. A：电影几点开始?

   Diànyǐng jǐ diǎn kāishǐ?

   When does the movie start?

   B：______________________。(7:10 pm)

四、实践汉语。

Practice your Chinese.

Before you make an appointment, ask the other party what his/her schedule is like and what time fits his / her best.

实用一点通

Cultural Tips

In general, most Chinese are punctual for appointment and they will arrive at the agreed place several minutes earlier. But when they are late, they will not give you detailed explanation and will generally say: "I'm sorry, I had something else to do." Please don't feel upset and think you deserve a more decent explanation. Actually, they are not proud of their being late, but feel sorry for keeping you waiting and will be even more so if they take time giving you their trivial explanation.

应变百宝囊

Language Enrichment

❶	上班	shàng bān	go to work
❷	下班	xià bān	be off duty
❸	秘书	mìshū	secretary
❹	联系	liánxì	contact
❺	预约	yùyuē	make a reservation/an appointment
❻	公司	gōngsī	company
❼	办公室	bàngōngshì	office
❽	文件	wénjiàn	file

Lesson 25

25

买票

Mǎi Piào

Buying Tickets

学习主题 Subject

During your stay in a place, buying ticket is an important activity, including movie tickets, theater tickets, tickets for parks and museums, as well as bus, train and air tickets. So it will be convenient for you if there are some common expressions for buying different tickets. Are there such expressions?

学习重点 Language Focus

重点词 Key Words and Phrases

❶ 票	piào	*n.*	ticket
❷ 买	mǎi	*v.*	buy
❸ 张	zhāng	*m.*	*for paper, desk, etc.*

重点句 Key Sentences

❶ 有……的票吗？

Yǒu……de piào ma?

Are there any tickets for…?

❷ 我买五张票。

Wǒ mǎi wǔ zhāng piào.

I want five tickets.

❸ 我买四月二十二号的票。

Wǒ mǎi sì yuè èrshí'èr hào de piào.

I want a ticket for April 22.

会话示例 Dialogues

I

[电影院售票处。]

小张：请问，有《野蛮师姐》的票吗？①

售票员：你看几点的？②

小张：4点10分的。

售票员：有。你要几张？

小张：我买两张。

售票员：六十块。

小张：给你。

售票员：给你票。

小张：谢谢。走吧。

[Diànyǐngyuàn shòupiàochù.]

Xiǎo Zhāng: Qǐngwèn, yǒu《Yěmán Shījiě》de piào ma?

Shòupiàoyuán: Nǐ kàn jǐ diǎn de?

Xiǎo Zhāng: Sì diǎn shí fēn de.

Shòupiàoyuán: Yǒu. Nǐ yào jǐ zhāng?

Xiǎo Zhāng: Wǒ mǎi liǎng zhāng.

Shòupiàoyuán: Liùshí kuài.

Xiǎo Zhāng: Gěi nǐ.

Shòupiàoyuán: Gěi nǐ piào.

Xiǎo Zhāng: Xièxie. Zǒu ba.

注释 Notes

I

[At the box office of a movie theater.]

Xiao Zhang: Excuse me, have you got any tickets for Windstruck?

Ticket agent: Which show do you want?

Xiao Zhang: The four ten one.

Ticket agent: Yes. How many tickets?

Xiao Zhang: Two, please.

Ticket agent: Sixty yuan.

Xiao Zhang: Here you are.

Ticket agent: Here're the tickets.

Xiao Zhang: Thanks. Let's go.

① We have learned "有……吗？" structure such as "这儿有公用电话吗？(Is there a public telephone nearby?)", "有可乐吗？(Do you have coke?)" etc. Then it is easy to understand "有……的票吗？(Do you have tickets for…?)" By filling in the blank with the title of the movie or play, the structure thus generated will be a question whether tickets for this movie or play are available. By filling in the blank with "去 + place", a question is asked about the availability of the tickets for a place.

② A：你看几点的（电影）？
B：（我看）4点10分的（电影）。

As the movie was mentioned before, the booking agent and Xiao Zhang left it out in their conversation. Similar omissions are common in Chinese such as the following conversation at a train ticket office:

A：有去成都的票吗？
Yǒu qù Chéngdū de piào ma?
Do you have tickets for Chengdu?

B：有，你要哪天的？
Yǒu, nǐ yào nǎ tiān de?
Yes, (tickets) for when?

A：九月十号的。
Jiǔ yuè shí hào de.
(Tickets) for September 10.

会话示例 Dialogues

Ⅱ

[小张在飞机票代售点买票。]

售票员：您好！

小张：你好！我要买票。③

售票员：您要去哪儿？

小张：去桂林。

售票员：哪④天的？

小张：四月二十二号的。

售票员：几张票？

小张：三张。

售票员：一共是三千六百二十一块。

小张：给你。

售票员：正好⑤，给您票。

小张：谢谢。

[Xiǎo Zhāng zài fēijīpiào dàishòudiǎn mǎi piào.]

Shòupiàoyuán: Nín hǎo!

Xiǎo Zhāng: Nǐ hǎo! Wǒ yào mǎi piào.

Shòupiàoyuán: Nín yào qù nǎr?

Xiǎo Zhāng: Qù Guìlín.

Shòupiàoyuán: Nǎ tiān de?

Xiǎo Zhāng: Sì yuè èrshí'èr hào de.

Shòupiàoyuán: Jǐ zhāng piào?

Xiǎo Zhāng: Sān zhāng.

Shòupiàoyuán: Yígòng shì sānqiān liùbǎi èrshíyī kuài.

Xiǎo Zhāng: Gěi nǐ.

Shòupiàoyuán: Zhèng hǎo, gěi nín piào.

Xiǎo Zhāng: Xièxie.

注释 Notes

II

[*Xiao Zhang is at a plane ticket agency.*]

Ticket agent: Can I help you?

Xiao Zhang: Hi, I'd like to have some tickets.

Ticket agent: Where to?

Xiao Zhang: Guilin.

Ticket agent: On which date?

Xiao Zhang: April 22.

Ticket agent: How many tickets?

Xiao Zhang: Three.

Ticket agent: 3,621 yuan altogether.

Xiao Zhang: Here you are.

Ticket agent: Ok, just the right amount. Here're the tickets.

Xiao Zhang: Thank you.

③ [我要买票] is used to start the conversation with the ticket clerk. You should state what ticket you need as well as the number of tickets you need, often in such pattern as "number of tickets + time + type of ticket", such as:

一张今晚八点的《神话》。
Yì zhāng jīn wǎn bā diǎn de《Shénhuà》.
One ticket for The Myth at 8:00 pm tonight.

两张二十五号到上海的机票。
Liǎng zhāng èrshíwǔ hào dào Shànghǎi de jīpiào.
Two air tickets to Shanghai on the 25th.

④ [哪] means "which" here. Apart from "哪天", you may also say "哪年 (which year)", "哪月 (which month)". "哪" may also be used with a measure word such as "哪个(which one)" and "哪位(which person)", where it is often pronounced as "něi" in spoken Chinese.

⑤ [正好] indicates the same amount as required by the ticket clerk. Normally, to avoid misunderstanding, the ticket clerk will say the amount paid by the customer and tell the customer the change aloud.

练习 Exercises

一、从右栏给左栏的词语找到相应的英文释义。

Match the Chinese expressions with the English ones.

票	piào	how many
点	diǎn	buy
买	mǎi	which
哪	nǎ	o'clock
几	jǐ	ticket

二、根据图画，使用合适的量词完成对话。

Complete the dialogues according to the pictures.

1. A：你喝绿茶还是花茶？

Nǐ hē lǜchá háishi huāchá?

Would you like green tea or scented tea?

B：我要一 ______ 绿茶。

Wǒ yào yì ______ lǜchá.

I'd like to have a ______ of green tea.

2. A：来一 ______ 牛奶怎么样？

Lái yì ______ niúnǎi zěnmeyàng?

How about a ______ of milk?

B：我今天想喝可乐。来一 ______ 可乐吧。

Wǒ jīntiān xiǎng hē kělè. Lái yì ______ kělè ba.

I'd like to have some coke today. A ______ of coke for me, please.

3. A：六百二十四块，正好。两 ______ 票，给你。

Liùbǎi èrshísì kuài, zhèng hǎo. Liǎng ______ piào, gěi nǐ.

624 yuan. Here are the two tickets.

B：谢谢。

Xièxie.

Thank you.

三、意念表达。

Express the following functions and notions.

1. You want to buy a ticket for the seven o'clock movie this evening.
2. Your parents and you are flying to Qingdao tomorrow. Get some tickets.

四、根据语境，完成对话。

Complete the dialogue according to the context.

1. (At the ticket office of a railway station.)

Ticket client: 你要去哪儿？

Nǐ yào qù nǎr?

Where to?

TOM: 去天津。

Qù Tiānjīn.

Tianjin.

Ticket client: 哪天的票？

Nǎ tiān de piào?

On which date?

TOM: ______________。

______________.

Ticket client: 你要几张？

Nǐ yào jǐ zhāng?

How many?

TOM: ______________。

______________.

Ticket client: 九月二号，两张，一共一百元。

Jiǔ yuè èr hào, liǎng zhāng, yígòng yìbǎi yuán.

OK, two tickets to Tianjin on September 2, 100 yuan, please.

2. (At the box office of a movie theater.)

TOM: 请问，______________？

Qǐngwèn, ______________?

Excuse me, ...

Ticket client: 有《神话》，你要几张？

Yǒu《Shénhuà》, nǐ yào jǐ zhāng?

Yes, we've got some tickets left for The Myth. How many do you want?

TOM: ______________。

______________.

Ticket client: 五张，一共三百元。

Wǔ zhāng, yígòng sānbǎi yuán.

Five tickets. 300 yuan in total please.

五、实践汉语。

Practice your Chinese.

You're planning a trip to Hangzhou on October 1, and would like to return to Beijing the 3rd. Call a ticket agency to book your tickets.

实用一点通
Cultural Tips

Generally you have to stand in a line to buy tickets in many places. But when a large crowd gathers in a limited space, body contact might be inevitable and someone else next to you might put a hand on your shoulder. Don't be upset if nobody apologies for it, for no offence is meant here.

应变百宝囊
Language Enrichment

各种各样的票
Various Tickets

❶	火车票	huǒchēpiào	train ticket
❷	软卧	ruǎnwò	soft sleeper
❸	硬卧	yìngwò	hard sleeper
❹	硬座	yìngzuò	hard seat
❺	飞机票	fēijīpiào	air ticket
❻	经济舱	jīngjìcāng	economy class
❼	头等舱	tóuděngcāng	first class
❽	往返票	wǎngfǎnpiào	return ticket
❾	联票	liánpiào	coupon ticket
❿	电影票	diànyǐngpiào	movie ticket
⓫	团体票	tuántǐpiào	group ticket
⓬	免票	miǎnpiào	free of charge
⓭	门票	ménpiào	admission ticket
⓮	船票	chuánpiào	steamer ticket
⓯	成人票	chéngrénpiào	adult ticket
⓰	儿童票	értóngpiào	child ticket

26
Lesson 26

打电话 I（找人）

Dǎ Diànhuà I (Zhǎo Rén)

Making a Phone Call

学习主题
Subject

To talk over the phone is an important way to communicate. With limited Chinese, how do you tell the one who picks up the phone on the other side to find the one you want to talk with? Find out here, and learn much more about telephone calling basics.

学习重点 Language Focus

重点词 Key Words and Phrases

1	喂	wèi	*int.*	hello
2	找	zhǎo	*v.*	look for
3	谁	shéi / shuí	*qp.*	who; whom
4	在	zài	*v.*	be at; be in
5	回	huí	*v.*	reply to (a phone call)
6	电话	diànhuà	*n.*	telephone

重点句 Key Sentences

1. 吕老师在吗?
   Lǚ lǎoshī zài ma?
   Is Ms. Lü in?

2. 喂，你好，你找谁?
   Wèi, nǐ hǎo, nǐ zhǎo shéi?
   Hello. Who do you wish to speak to?

3. 你是哪儿/哪位?
   Nǐ shì nǎr/nǎ wèi?
   Who's that?

4. 电话是……
   Diànhuà shì……
   My telephone number is…

5. 请他给我回电话，好吗?
   Qǐng tā gěi wǒ huí diànhuà, hǎo ma?
   Could you please ask him to call me back when he returns?

会话示例 Dialogues

I

大乔：喂①！

小张：喂，大乔，我是小张。

大乔：哦，小张，你好！

Dà Qiáo: Wèi!

Xiǎo Zhāng: Wèi, Dà Qiáo, wǒ shì Xiǎo Zhāng.

Dà Qiáo: Ò, Xiǎo Zhāng, nǐ hǎo!

II

杨琴：喂，你好，你找谁②？

梁辉：我找吕老师，她在吗？

杨琴：在，您稍等。吕老师，电话。

吕老师：喂，你好，你是哪位③？

梁辉：您好！吕老师，我是梁辉。

吕老师：哦，你好！

Yáng Qín: Wèi, nǐ hǎo, nǐ zhǎo shéi?

Liáng Huī: Wǒ zhǎo Lǚ lǎoshī, tā zài ma?

Yáng Qín: Zài, nín shāo děng. Lǚ lǎoshī, diànhuà.

Lǚ lǎoshī: Wèi, nǐ hǎo! Nǐ shì nǎ wèi?

Liáng Huī: Nín hǎo! Lǚ lǎoshī, wǒ shì Liáng Huī.

Lǚ lǎoshī: Ò, nǐ hǎo!

注释 Notes

I

Da Qiao: Hello.

Xiao Zhang: Hello, Da Qiao. This is Xiao Zhang.

Da Qiao: Hi, Xiao Zhang. How are you?

II

Yang Qin: Hello. Who are you calling for?

Liang Hui: I'd like to speak to Ms. Lü . Is she in?

Yang Qin: Yes. Hold on for a moment. Ms. Lü, it's for you.

Ms. Lü: Hello. Who's that?

Liang Hui: Hello, Ms. Lü, it's for you. This is Liang Hui.

Ms. Lü: Hi. How are you?

① [喂] is the Chinese equivalent of "Hello". It is the first word to say when you make or answer a phone call. As "喂" is only meant to attract the other party's attention, it would be polite to add a "你好" after it. Another thing to note is that even though the word is marked with a fourth tone "wèi" in the Chinese dictionary, it is usually pronounced in the second tone "wéi" to show more intimacy with the other party.

② Once the call is connected, the calling party should tell the receiving party whom he or she wishes to speak to. If the calling party fails to do so, the receiving party may well ask a question like "你找谁？ (who do you wish to speak to?)".

③ In Chinese, the calling party is expected to identify him or herself first. If the calling party fails to do so, the receiving party may well ask a question like "你是哪位？ (Who's that?)" or "你是哪儿？(Who's calling?)" This is especially true for private calls. The literal translation for "哪儿" is "where". However, the other party is not interested in knowing where you are, he or she just wants to know who you are.

会话示例 Dialogues

III

A: 你好！
B: 请问，王浩在吗？④
A: 他不在，他出去了。
B: 哦，他回来后，请他给⑤我回电话，好吗？
A: 好的。
B: 我的电话是66848112⑥。
A: 66848112。好的，再见。
B: 谢谢，再见。

A: Nǐ hǎo!
B: Qǐngwèn, Wáng Hào zài ma?
A: Tā bú zài, tā chūqu le.
B: Ò, Tā huílai hòu, qǐng tā gěi wǒ huí diànhuà, hǎo ma?
A: Hǎo de.
B: Wǒ de diànhuà shì liù liù bā sì bā yāo yāo èr.
A: Liù liù bā sì bā yāo yāo èr. Hǎo de, zàijiàn.
B: Xièxie, zàijiàn.

注释 Notes

III

A: Hello!

B: Excuse me. Is Wang Hao in?

A: Sorry, he's not in. He's just left.

B: Oh. Could you please ask him to call me back when he returns?

A: Sure.

B: My telephone number is 66848112.

A: 66848112. OK. Goodbye.

B: Thanks! Bye-bye.

④ [王浩在吗？] means "Is Wang Hao at home/in the office?" If you are calling his home, "在" refers to "at home", and if you are calling his office, "在" refers to "in the office". Regardless of where the person you wish to speak to is, you may ask "××在吗？(Is ×× in?)" as long as you have the right number.

⑤ [给] is the equivalent of "to" or "for". "给" is used to introduce the object of the verb using the pattern: "给＋sb.＋v-phrase". For instance,

给我回电话。
Gěi wǒ huí diànhuà.
Call me back.
给他打电话。
Gěi tā dǎ diànhuà.
Call him.

⑥ In China, the number of digits in a telephone number depends on the size of the city. At present, metropolises like Beijing, Tianjin and Shanghai have 8-digit telephone numbers, while other cities have 7-digit numbers. Cell phones usually have 11-digit numbers.

练习 Exercises

一、从右栏给左栏的词语找到相应的英文释义。

Match the Chinese expressions with the English ones.

找	zhǎo	again
打	dǎ	o'clock
点	diǎn	after
后	hòu	speak to
再	zài	call

二、意念表达。

Express the following functions and notions.

1. You wish to speak to Mr. Li. Make a telephone call to him.
2. Leave your telephone number with Xiao Wang's co-worker, and ask him or her to tell Xiao Wang to call you back.

三、下面是几个打电话的片段，请根据语境完成对话。

The following are segments of several telephone conversations. Please complete the dialogues according to the proper context.

1. A：喂，你好，你找谁？

   Wèi, nǐ hǎo, nǐ zhǎo shéi?

   Hello. Who do you wish to speak to?

   B：____________________。

   A：小王啊，请稍等。

   Xiǎo Wáng a, qǐng shāo děng.

   Ah, Xiao Wang. A moment, please.

2. A：________________。

B：喂，你好。

Wèi, nǐ hǎo.

Hello.

A：________________？

B：小张不在。

Xiǎo Zhāng bú zài.

Xiao Zhang is not in.

3. A：那就这样吧。

Nà jiù zhèyàng ba.

Then let's settle it this way.

B：________________。

A：再见！

Zàijiàn!

Goodbye.

四、实践汉语。

Practice your Chinese.

You want to see a movie during the weekend with your good friend, Xiao Zhang, whom you haven't seen for a long time. Call him to make an appointment with him.

实用一点通

Cultural Tips

Calling someone is usually not as smoothly as one expected. Sometimes the one you call is not available, then you would want to leave a message for him/her with the one who answers the phone. So it's important that you remember your own phone number in Chinese and be sure to tell the one answering the phone, so that the one you want to talk to will call you back later.

应变百宝囊

Language Enrichment

❶	免费	miǎnfèi	free of charge
❷	留言	liú yán	leave a message
❸	查询	cháxún	inquire
❹	区号	qūhào	arca codc
❺	总机	zǒngjī	switchboard (number)
❻	分机	fēnjī	extension (number)
❼	电话卡	diànhuàkǎ	telephone card
❽	话费	huàfèi	telephone rate; charge
❾	国内长途	guónèi chángtú	DDD
❿	国际长途	guójì chángtú	IDD
⓫	市内电话	shìnèi diànhuà	local call

27

Lesson 27

打电话 II（转接电话）

Dǎ Diànhuà II (Zhuǎn Jiē Diànhuà)

Transferring a Phone Call

学习主题
Subject

You and your friend are on a trip somewhere. You've gone out alone and want to call your friend back in the hotel. You find a public pay phone, call the hotel operator first and tell him/her to put you through to a particular room or extension number. You'll learn how to make it work here.

学习重点 Language Focus

重点词 Key Words and Phrases

❶	转	zhuǎn	*v.*	transfer
❷	告（诉）	gào (su)	*v.*	tell
❸	一定	yídìng	*adv.*	must; certainly
❹	没（有）	méi (yǒu)	*v.*	have not; not yet
❺	人	rén	*n.*	person
❻	接	jiē	*v.*	receive

重点句 Key Sentences

❶ 哪儿有电话？

Nǎr yǒu diànhuà?

Where can I find a telephone?

❷ 请转……

Qǐng zhuǎn……

Please transfer the line to …

❸ 请转告/告诉他……

Qǐng zhuǎngào/gàosu tā……

Please tell him…

会话示例 Dialogues

I

A: 你好！请问，这儿哪儿有电话？①
B: 在那儿。
A: 谢谢。
B: 不客气。

A: Nǐ hǎo! Qǐngwèn, zhèr nǎr yǒu diànhuà?
B: Zài nàr.
A: Xièxie.
B: Bú kèqi.

II

A: 喂！
B: 喂，你好，是张先生家吗？
A: 是的，他不在。
B: 哦，对不起，你是……
A: 我是他爱人②。
B: 哦，你好！我是陈洁。请你转告他，我明天早上7点到上海。
A: 好的，我一定告诉他。
B: 谢谢你。

A: Wèi!
B: Wèi, nǐ hǎo, shì Zhāng xiānsheng jiā ma?
A: Shì de, tā bú zài.
B: Ò, duìbuqǐ, nǐ shì……
A: Wǒ shì tā àiren.
B: Ò, nǐ hǎo! Wǒ shì Chén Jié. Qǐng nǐ zhuǎngào tā, wǒ míngtiān zǎoshang qī diǎn dào Shànghǎi.
A: Hǎo de, wǒ yídìng gàosu tā.
B: Xièxie nǐ.

注释 Notes

I

A: Excuse me, where can I find a telephone?

B: There's one over there.

A: Thanks.

B: You're welcome.

II

A: Hello.

B: Hello. Is this Mr. Zhang's residence?

A: Yes, but he's not in now.

B: Oh, and this is…

A: This is his wife.

B: Oh, hi, this is Chen Jie. Could you please tell him that I'm arriving in Shanghai at seven tomorrow morning?

A: Sure. I'll tell him.

B: Thank you.

① When you are out, you may need to use a local public phone. Public phones in China are available in two types: attended or unattended. Attended phones often carry a sign of public phone. What is good about this type of public phone is you do not have to have coins or phone cards, and you may get help from the people who attend to the phone in time of trouble. Unattended phones come in two categories: the coin pay phone and the card pay phone. You operate a coin pay phone by paying five jiao per call for a duration of three minutes. Phone cards are available for sale at hotels, newspaper-stands and department stores. Or you may ask:

哪儿卖电话卡?

Nǎr mài diànhuàkǎ?

Where can I buy a phone card?

② No matter male or female, a Chinese will refer to his/her spouse as "我爱人" meaning "my spouse", or "my wife" for a man and "my husband" for a woman.

会话示例 Dialogues

III

[办公室里，小张拨电话。]

服务员：你好！香江酒店。

小张：你好！请转20101③。

服务员：好，请稍等。

……

对不起，电话没人接。

小张：那，请转20102。

服务员：好，请稍等。

[Bàngōngshì li, Xiǎo Zhāng bō diànhuà.]

Fúwùyuán: Nǐ hǎo! Xiāngjiāng Jiǔdiàn.

Xiǎo Zhāng: Nǐ hǎo! Qǐng zhuǎn èr líng yāo líng yāo.

Fúwùyuán: Hǎo, qǐng shāo děng.

……

Duìbuqǐ, diànhuà méi rén jiē.

Xiǎo Zhāng: Nà, qǐng zhuǎn èr líng yāo líng èr.

Fúwùyuán: Hǎo, qǐng shāo děng.

注释 Notes

III

[Xiao Zhang is making a phone call in his office.]

Operator: Hello, Xiangjiang Hotel. May I help you?

Xiao Zhang: Hello. Extension 20101, please.

Operator: OK, just a moment ...

Sorry, nobody's in.

Xiao Zhang: Then 20102 please.

Operator: Sure, a moment, please.

③ If you are to dial an extension, you may ask the operator to connect you by saying "请转……" after you reach the switchboard. If you do not know the extension number, you may say "请转……号房间 (please transfer me to Room No....)" as normally room numbers are extension numbers at some hotels although some require an additional number before the room number.

练习 Exercises

一、从右栏给左栏的词语找到相应的英文释义。

Match the Chinese words with the English ones.

电话	diànhuà	people
告诉	gàosu	receive
人	rén	transfer
接	jiē	telephone
转	zhuǎn	tell

二、意念表达。

Express the following functions and notions.

1. Ask the person who answers the phone to tell Lao Wang that you're arriving in Beijing at eight tomorrow morning.
2. Call Mr. Zhang who stays in Room 1021 of Beijing Hotel.

三、选择合适的词语，完成对话。

Choose the proper words to complete the dialogues.

A. 接 jiē pick up　　B. 打 dǎ dial　　C. 回 huí call back　　D. 转 zhuǎn transfer

1. 甲：你好，请__________6032。
   Nǐ hǎo, qǐng __________ 6032.
   Hello, extension 6032 please.
   乙：好，请稍等。
   Hǎo, qǐng shāo děng.
   Sure, a moment please.
2. 甲：他有事刚出去。
   Tā yǒu shì gāng chūqu.
   He's just left.
   乙：他回来后，请他给我__________电话，好吗？
   Tā huílai hòu, qǐng tā gěi wǒ __________diànhuà, hǎo ma?
   Could you please tell him to call me back when he returns?

四、根据语境，完成对话。

Complete the dialogue according to the context.

1. A：我想打电话，请问，__________？
   Wǒ xiǎng dǎ diànhuà, qǐngwèn, __________?
   Excuse me, I want to make a phone call, but ...

B：在那儿。
Zài nàr.
It's over there.

2. A：你好！是北京饭店吗？
Nǐ hǎo! Shì Běijīng Fàndiàn ma?
Hello. Is that Beijing Hotel?

B：是的。
Shì de.
Yes.

A：＿＿＿＿＿＿。
＿＿＿＿＿＿.

B：2011转接中，请稍等。
Èr líng yāo yāo zhuǎnjiē zhong, qǐng shāo děng.
I'll put you through 2011. A moment, please.

五、实践汉语。

Practice your Chinese.

Call the Consumers' Association to file a complaint against a seller and leave your contact information.

实用一点通
Cultural Tips

When you are away from the hotel and want to call your friend back at the hotel, you first need know the room number of your friend, for the hotel operator will ask either for the room number or for the extension number. Most hotels will use room numbers as the extension numbers, so after reaching the hotel operator, plesse tell him/her "请转" plus the extension number.

应变百宝囊
Language Enrichment

常用电话
Useful Telephone Numbers

❶ 匪警台	police emergency number	110
❷ 火警台	fire emergency number	119
❸ 医疗急救台	medical emergency number	120/999
❹ 民航信息查询台	inquiry center for civil aviation	962580
❺ 铁路信息查询台	inquiry center for railway information	962585

28 Lesson 28

生 病

Shēng Bìng

Seeing a Doctor

学习主题 Subject

Chinese always say that everyone living on grains will be ill sometime. When you feel sick and need to see a doctor, what would you say to your friends and how would you describe your symptoms to your doctor?

学习重点 Language Focus

重点词 Key Words and Phrases

❶	怎么	zěnme	*qp.*	how; why
❷	肚子	dùzi	*n.*	stomach
❸	疼	téng	*adj.*	ache
❹	看病	kàn bìng	*v.*	see a doctor
❺	舒服	shūfu	*adj.*	comfortable
❻	头	tóu	*n.*	head
❼	发烧	fā shāo	*v.*	have a fever
❽	觉得	juéde	*v.*	feel
❾	冷	lěng	*adj.*	cold

重点句 Key Sentences

❶ 你怎么了？
Nǐ zěnme le?
What's wrong with you?

❷ 你哪儿不舒服？
Nǐ nǎr bù shūfu?
What's wrong with you?

❸ 我觉得很冷。
Wǒ juéde hěn lěng.
I feel cold.

❹ 我头疼。
Wǒ tóuténg.
I've got a headache.

❺ 我肚子疼。
Wǒ dùzi téng.
I've got a stomachache.

❻ 我要看病。
Wǒ yào kàn bìng.
I need to see a doctor.

会话示例 Dialogues

I

[一个男人捂着肚子。]

A：你怎么了①？

B：我肚子疼，我要看病。

[Yí ge nánrén wǔzhe dùzi.]

A: Nǐ zěnme le?

B: Wǒ dùzi téng, wǒ yào kàn bìng.

II

[一个女人在揉胳膊。]

A：你哪儿不舒服？

B：我这儿疼。

[Yí ge nǚrén zài róu gēbo.]

A: Nǐ nǎr bù shūfu?

B: Wǒ zhèr téng.

III

[琳琳趴在桌子上。]

同事：琳琳怎么了？你哪儿不舒服？

琳琳：我头疼。

[同事摸琳琳的头。]

同事：哟，你发烧了。

琳琳：可能有点儿，我觉得②很冷。

[Línlin pā zài zhuōzi shang.]

Tóngshì: Línlin zěnme le? Nǐ nǎr bù shūfu?

Línlin: Wǒ tóuténg.

[Tóngshì mō Línlin de tóu.]

Tóngshì: Yō, nǐ fā shāo le.

Línlin: Kěnéng yǒudiǎnr, wǒ juéde hěn lěng.

注释 Notes

I

[*A man covers his stomach with his hands in agony.*]

A: What's wrong with you?

B: I have a stomachache. I need to see a doctor.

II

[*A woman is massaging her arm.*]

A: What's wrong with you?

B: It hurts here.

III

[*Linlin bends over her desk .*]

Colleague: What' wrong with you, Linlin? Are you feeling unwell?

Linlin: I have a headache.

[*A colleague feels her head.*]

Colleague: Oh, you are running a fever.

Linlin: Perhaps. I feel cold.

① When your friend finds you unwell, he/she may ask "你怎么了" ,which literally means "what's wrong with you". He/she asks because he/she cares about you. In response to that, you may tell him/her directly how you feel. If you don't want to tell him/her, you may say "没关系" "没事儿" , meaning "I'm all right. I'm OK." But if you really fall ill or feel unwell and have had that illness before, you'd better tell your friends and go to see a doctor. "哪儿不舒服" and "怎么了" are almost of the same meaning, with "舒服" meaning "comfortable".

② [觉得] can be used to refer to two different kinds of feelings. One is the physical feeling just like the case in the dialogue where "觉得" means "feel" and is followed by an adjective. The other is the psychological feeling.

When one expresses his/her opinions, he/she often starts by saying "我觉得" meaning "I think". In this case, "觉得" is followed by a sentence, for instance,

我觉得他是个好人。
Wǒ juéde tā shì ge hǎorén.
I think he is a good guy.

练习 Exercises

一、从右栏给左栏的汉语找到相应的英文释义。

Match the Chinese expressions with the English ones.

舒服	shūfu	ache
冷	lěng	have a fever
疼	téng	see a doctor
发烧	fā shāo	comfortable
看病	kàn bìng	cold

二、根据英文提示连线，并用汉语说出正确的句子。

Match the words or expressions in the three columns and make sentences based on the English.

1.

小张 Xiǎo Zhāng	觉得有点儿 juéde yǒudiǎnr	不舒服 bù shūfu
我 wǒ		头疼 tóuténg
他 tā		冷 lěng

He feels he has a mild headache.

____

Xiao Zhang feels somewhat cold.

____

I feel a little unwell.

____

2.

老王 Lǎo Wáng 她 tā	头 tóu 肚子 dùzi	有点儿 yǒudiǎnr 很 hěn 不 bù	疼 téng

Lao Wang has got a severe headache.

____

Her stomach aches a little.

____

三、根据语境，完成对话。

Complete the dialogues according to the context.

1. A：__________________？

   B：我有点儿不舒服。

   Wǒ yǒudiǎnr bù shūfu.

   I feel a bit unwell.

2. A：__________________。（冷 lěng）

   B：你可能发烧了。

   Nǐ kěnéng fā shāo le.

   You might have a fever.

3. A：我不拉肚子，__________________。（恶心 ěxin）

   Wǒ bù lā dùzi, __________________.

   I don't have loose bowels, but...

   B：你可能感冒了，我送你去医院吧。

   Nǐ kěnéng gǎnmào le, wǒ sòng nǐ qù yīyuàn ba.

   You might have a cold. I'll accompany you to the hospital.

四、实践汉语。

Practice your Chinese.

1. You can't take spicy food, but couldn't resist the temptation and ate a lot when having dinner with your Chinese friend yesterday. When your friend calls you and asks how you are doing, what would you say?
2. Your friend feels unwell. Ask him/her what's wrong and offer your help.

实用一点通 Cultural Tips

When one is away from home alone, the top fear is being sick, especially in a foreign country. If you suffer certain chronic disease, please ask your doctor back at home to prescribe sufficient medicine and to inform you of the name of the disease. You'd better have the name translated into Chinese and put it down in a card so that you can take it with you when you travel in China. In case the illness comes on, this will help the local doctor to conclude with an accurate diagnosis and treatment. In general, you can use simple Chinese to tell your symptoms to the doctor, including "这儿疼", "这儿痒", and "这儿不舒服".

应变百宝囊 Language Enrichment

❶ 流鼻涕	liú bíti	have a runny nose
❷ 过敏	guòmǐn	be allergic
❸ 恶心	ěxin	feel like vomiting

4	呕吐	ǒutù	vomit
5	头晕	tóu yūn	dizzy
6	咳嗽	késou	cough
7	便秘	biànmì	constipation
8	发炎	fāyán	have inflammation
9	消化不良	xiāohuà bù liáng	indigestion
10	胃口	wèikǒu	appetite
11	失眠	shī mián	have insomnia
12	嗓子	sǎngzi	throat

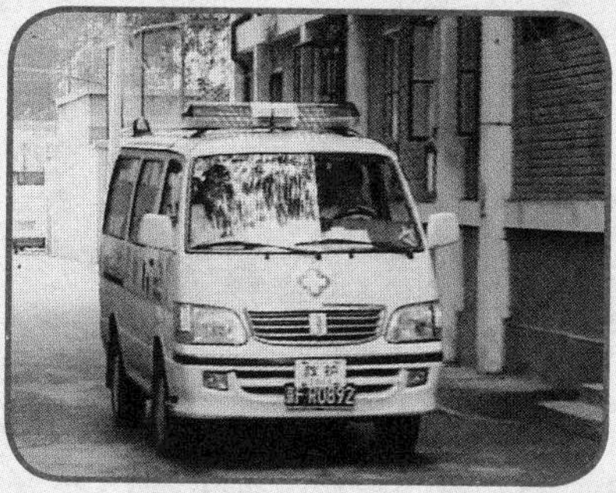

29

Lesson 29

买药

Mǎi Yào

Buying Medicine

学习主题
Subject

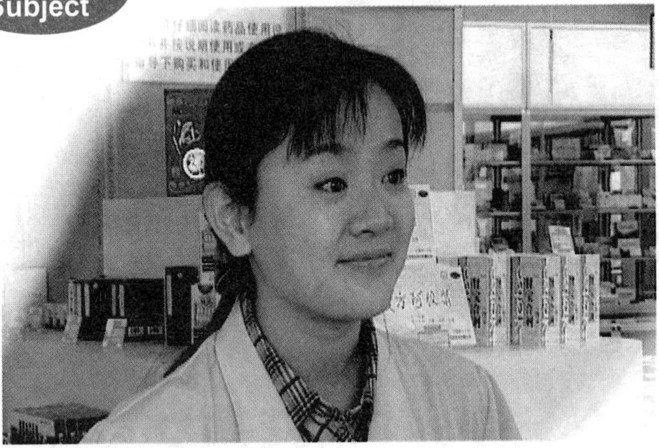

Find out the difference between Chinese drug stores and the ones you are familiar with back at home and learn how to get the medicines you need here.

学习重点 Language Focus

重点词 Key Words and Phrases

1	感冒	gǎnmào	*v.*	have a cold
2	医院	yīyuàn	*n.*	hospital
3	药	yào	*n.*	medicine
4	消炎	xiāo yán	*v.*	diminish inflammation
5	嗓子	sǎngzi	*n.*	throat
6	咳嗽	késou	*v.*	cough

重点句 Key Sentences

1. 有感冒药吗？
   Yǒu gǎnmào yào ma?
   Do you have any medicine for cold?

2. 我要消炎药。
   Wǒ yào xiāoyán yào.
   I want some medicine to diminish inflammation.

3. 有没有咳嗽药？
   Yǒu méiyǒu késou yào?
   Do you have any medicine for cough?

4. 我不想去医院。
   Wǒ bù xiǎng qù yīyuàn.
   I don't want to go to the hospital.

5. 吃点儿药就行了。
   Chī diǎnr yào jiù xíng le.
   Some medicine will do.

会话示例 Dialogues

I

[办公室里，琳琳感觉不太舒服。]

同事：你可能①感冒了②。我们送你去医院吧。

琳琳：我不想去医院。吃点儿感冒药就行了③。

同事：那我们送你回家吧。

琳琳：好的。

[Bàngōngshì li, Línlin gǎnjué bú tài shūfu.]

Tóngshì: Nǐ kěnéng gǎnmào le, wǒmen sòng nǐ qù yīyuàn ba.

Línlin: Wǒ bù xiǎng qù yīyuàn. Chī diǎnr gǎnmào yào jiù xíng le.

Tóngshì: Nà wǒmen sòng nǐ huí jiā ba.

Línlin: Hǎo de.

注释　Notes

I

[*In the office, Linlin doesn't feel well.*]

Colleague:
You might have a cold. Let me take you to the hospital.

Linlin: I don't want to go to the hospital. Some medicine will do.

Colleague:
We'll take you home then.

Linlin: OK.

① [可能] indicates possibility. If you are quite certain about the case in question, you may say "很可能" meaning "very likely". If you are to express impossibility, you may say "不可能".

② [怎么了], [发烧了] and [感冒了] all have a "了", a particle which is indicative of something that has happened.

③ [……就行] means "...is OK", which is normally put at the end of a sentence to indicate as long as a certain condition is met, everything is OK. In addition, some Chinese often refrain from going to hospital for such malaise as cold and diarrhea, rather they go to drugstores to buy some medicine to pull through. Generally speaking, some common diseases can be cured by taking some ready-made herbal medicine as instructed.

会话示例 Dialogues

II

[药店里。]

A: 你好，有消炎药吗？

B: 有，你哪儿不舒服？

A: 我嗓子疼。

B: 这个药比较④好。

A: 有没有⑤咳嗽药⑥？

B: 有，给你这个。

A: 一共多少钱？

B: 三十二块。

A: 谢谢。

B: 不客气。

[Yàodiàn li.]

A: Nǐ hǎo, yǒu xiāoyán yào ma?

B: Yǒu, nǐ nǎr bù shūfu?

A: Wǒ sǎngzi téng.

B: Zhège yào bǐjiào hǎo.

A: Yǒu méiyǒu késou yào?

B: Yǒu, gěi nǐ zhège.

A: Yígòng duōshao qián?

B: Sānshí'èr kuài.

A: Xièxie.

B: Bú kèqi.

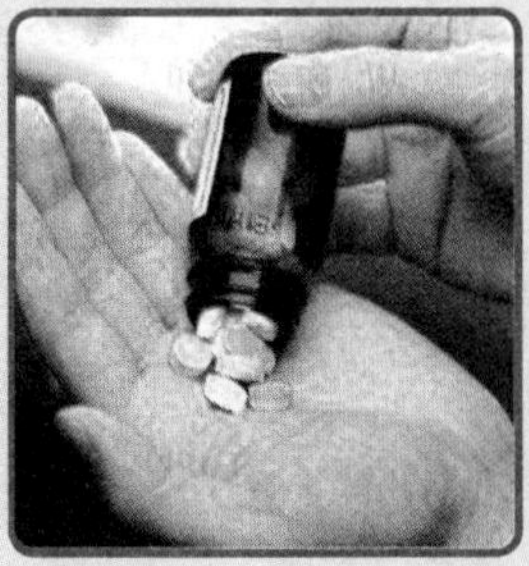

注释 Notes

II

[*At a drugstore.*]

A: Excuse me, do you have any medicine that diminishes inflammation?

B: Yes, we do. May I ask what's wrong with you?

A: I have a sore throat.

B: This medicine works well.

A: Do you have any medicine for cough?

B: Yes, here you are.

A: How much is the total?

B: Thirty-two yuan.

A: Thank you.

B: You are welcome.

④ [比较] means "relatively", which is often put before adjectives. In this case, salespersons won't use such extreme terms as "非常" or "很", both meaning "very", whereas "比较" is much more moderate.

⑤ [有没有……？] and [有……吗？] have the same meaning and function, meaning "Are there any…?" If you are looking for something in a department store, a restaurant, a book store or a drugstore, you may use either of these two patterns.

⑥ [咳嗽药] and [感冒药] seem to have the same structure as "消炎药" (anti-biotics), but they should be called "治咳嗽的药" and "治感冒的药", where "治" means "cure". Therefore, "治……的药" forms a structure where name of diseases is inserted to indicate the medicine to cure such a disease.

练习 Exercises

一、从右栏给左栏的汉语找到相应的英文释义。

Match the Chinese expressions with the English ones.

感冒	gǎnmào		medicine
咳嗽	késou		comfortable
消炎	xiāoyán		send
医院	yīyuàn		cough
舒服	shūfu		have a cold
药	yào		diminish inflammation
送	sòng		hospital

二、根据英文提示，把下面的词语组成一句话。

Make sentences with the given words.

1. Where is the hospital?

____

医院 哪儿 有
yīyuàn nǎr yǒu

2. How do I take the medicine?

____

药 怎么 这 吃
yào zěnme zhè chī

3. I need some medicine for cold.

____

感冒 要 我 药
gǎnmào yào wǒ yào

三、选择最合适的选项完成对话。

Choose the proper answer to complete the dialogue.

A. 我要感冒药。
Wǒ yào gǎnmào yào.
I need some medicine for cold.

B. 这药怎么吃？
Zhè yào zěnme chī?
How do I take the medicine?

C. 哪儿有药店？
Nǎr yǒu yàodiàn?
Where can I find a drugstore?

D. 三十二块。
Sānshí'èr kuài.
Thirty-two yuan.

1. A：你要什么药？
Nǐ yào shénme yào?
What medicine do you need?
B：________________

2. A：________________
B：一次一片。
Yí cì yí piàn.
A tablet each time.

3. A：一共多少钱？
Yígòng duōshao qián?
How much is it altogether?
B：________________

4. A：________________
B：一直走，然后往左拐，有一个。
Yìzhí zǒu, ránhòu wǎng zuǒ guǎi, yǒu yí ge.
There's one nearby. Just keep walking and turn left.

四、实践汉语。

Practice your Chinese.

A friend who travels with you in China suddenly has got a stomachache, and he doesn't know any Chinese. Try to help him out.

实用一点通
Cultural Tips

The drugs sold in a local drugstore fall roughly into two categories: drugs on prescription and OTC drugs. You have to have a prescription to get the former ones, while the latter ones are available for everyone. You can bring the package of the medicine you take regularly to show it to the pharmacist at the store or remember the Latin name of the medicine to search for it at the store yourself. Generally, most Western medicines are required to be prescribed by a doctor, while most Chinese traditional medicines are OTC. Since these medicines are made from traditional Chinese prescriptions that have been proved effective through hundreds of years of practice, most Chinese tend to favor these OTC medicines in daily life.

应变百宝囊
Language Enrichment

❶	胶囊	jiāonáng	capsule
❷	含片	hánpiàn	lozenge
❸	冲剂	chōngjì	instant herbal mixture
❹	打针	dǎ zhēn	give or take an injection
❺	药丸	yàowán	pill
❻	膏药	gāoyao	plaster
❼	体温	tǐwēn	body temperature
❽	血压	xuèyā	blood pressure
❾	流血	liú xiě	bleed
❿	胃疼	wèi téng	stomachache

30 Lesson 30

可以问的问题

Kěyǐ Wèn de Wèntí

Asking Proper Questions

学习主题 Subject

Since different countries have different cultures, you need to learn about Chinese culture so as to stick to appropriate topics when you have conversation with Chinese.

学习重点 Language Focus

重点词 Key Words and Phrases

1	身体	shēntǐ	*n.*	(human) body
2	多大	duō dà	*qp.*	how old
3	年纪	niánjì	*n.*	age
4	孩子	háizi	*n.*	child
5	结婚	jié hūn	*v.*	marry
6	好	hǎo	*adj.*	well

重点句 Key Sentences

1. 你多大了？

   Nǐ duō dà le?

   How old are you?

2. 您多大年纪了？

   Nín duō dà niánjì le?

   How old are you?

3. 你肚子好了吗？

   Nǐ dùzi hǎole ma?

   Has your stomach got better?

4. 看起来好多了。

   Kàn qǐlai hǎoduō le.

   It seems that it's got much better.

会话示例 Dialogues

I

A：您看起来①身体真好。您多大年纪了？②

B：我六十三岁了，身体还可以吧。

A: Nín kàn qǐlai shēntǐ zhēn hǎo. Nín duō dà niánjì le?

B: Wǒ liùshísān suì le, shēntǐ hái kěyǐ ba.

II

A：王华，你多大了？

B：我三十三岁。

A：你的孩子多大了？

B：老师，我还没结婚呢。

A：对不起。

B：没什么。

A: Wáng Huá, nǐ duō dà le?

B: Wǒ sānshísān suì.

A: Nǐ de háizi duō dà le?

B: Lǎoshī, wǒ hái méi jié hūn ne.

A: Duìbuqǐ.

B: Méi shénme.

III

[探望病人。]

A：我来看看你，你肚子好了吗？

B：好多了③，谢谢！

A：给你。

B：谢谢你，太客气了！

[Tànwàng bìngrén.]

A: Wǒ lái kànkan nǐ, nǐ dùzi hǎole ma?

B: Hǎo duō le, xièxie!

A: Gěi nǐ.

B: Xièxie nǐ, tài kèqi le!

注释 Notes

I

A: You look great! How old are you, if you don't mind my asking?

B: No, not at all. I'm sixty-three, and doing pretty well.

II

A: Wang Hua, how old are you?

B: I'm thirty-three.

A: How old is your kid?

B: I'm not married yet, Sir.

A: Oh, I'm sorry.

B: It's OK.

III

[*Visiting a patient.*]

A: How are you? Has your stomach got better?

B: Much better. Thank you!

A: Here you are.

B: Thanks a lot. It's very kind of you!

① [起来] in [看起来] does not mean "get up". It is used after a verb to indicate an estimation. Similar expressions are "听起来(sounds like)" and "闻起来(smells like)".

② [您多大年纪了？] is used to ask about the age of a senior person. "您" is a polite form to address someone. "你多大了？" can be used to ask about the age of an adult or a child. In addition, for a kid under 10, you may ask "你几岁了？". Here "几" means "how many" and "岁" means "age". The three questions above carry the same meaning "How old are you?", yet they are used to address different groups of people. Also, in China, sometimes you may ask women about their age.

③ [好多了] means much better than before in terms of the condition of the stomach. In Chinese, we often use "……多了" to indicate comparison, such as,

> 他看起来老多了。
> Tā kàn qǐlai lǎoduō le.
> He looks much older.

练习 Exercises

一、在右栏给左栏的词语找到相应的英文释义。

Match the Chinese words with the English ones.

身体	shēntǐ	child
年纪	niánjì	belly
孩子	háizi	marry
肚子	dùzi	(human) body; health
结婚	jié hūn	age

二、根据英文提示，把下面的词语连成一句话。

Make sentences with the given words.

1. How old are you?

____

多 duō　您 nín　了 le　大 dà　年纪 niánjì

2. Has your stomach got better?

____

肚子 dùzi　好 hǎo　了 le　吗 ma　你 nǐ

三、根据图示，完成对话。

Make dialogues based on the pictures.

1. A：______________________

B：我六十五岁了。

Wǒ liùshíwǔ suì le.

I'm sixty-five.

2\. A: ____________________

B：我十二岁了。

Wǒ shí'èr suì le.

I'm twelve.

四、实践汉语。

Practice your Chinese.

You visit a nursing home in China and have a chat with some senior citizens. Ask how old they are and how they are doing.

实用一点通 Cultural Tips

“请问” is an extremely useful expression apart from making your request or enquiry politely. In addition, if your oral Chinese is not fluent, to begin your enquiry with “请问” will make your intention clear to others. For example, if you want to know where the WC is, even if you simplify your question down to four characters of “请问，厕所？”, a Chinere can understand you.

应变百宝囊 Language Enrichment

❶ 您有几个孩子？
Nín yǒu jǐ ge háizi?
How many kids do you have?

❷ 你在哪儿工作？
Nǐ zài nǎr gōngzuò?
Where do you work?

❸ 你结婚了吗？
Nǐ jiē hūn le ma?
Are you married?

❹ 您休过假了吗？
Nín xiūguo jià le ma?
Have you taken your holidays?

❺ 您的名字怎么写/拼？
Nín de míngzi zěnme xiě/pīn?
How do you write/spell your name?

❻ 您介绍一下这里，好吗？
Nín jièshào yíxià zhèli, hǎo ma?
Can you say a few words about this place?

31
Lesson 31

不必介意的问题

Búbì Jièyì de Wèntí

Answering Embarrassing Questions

学习主题
Subject

A harmonious relationship between people with different cultural backgrounds is based on mutual understanding of differences. You might face some awkward or even difficult questions from your Chinese friends. Learn the skills to cope with such a situation.

学习重点 Language Focus

重点词 Key Words and Phrases

❶	叫	jiào	*v.*	be called
❷	名字	míngzi	*n.*	name
❸	老外	lǎowài	*n.*	foreigner
❹	国	guó	*n.*	nation; country
❺	人	rén	*n.*	person; people
❻	工作	gōngzuò	*n.*	job
❼	工资	gōngzī	*n.*	wage

重点句 Key Sentences

❶ 你是哪国人？

Nǐ shì nǎ guó rén?

Which country are you from?

❷ 不多，不多。

Bù duō, bù duō.

Not much.

❸ 你做什么工作？

Nǐ zuò shénme gōngzuò?

What's your job?

会话示例 Dialogues

I

[王小姐家。]

Sherry：你好啊！

默默：你好！

Sherry：你叫默默，是吗？

默默：是啊，你呢，你叫什么名字？①

Sherry：我叫Sherry，我没有中国名字。

默默：你是美国人吗？

Sherry：不是，我是加拿大人。

王小姐：来，喝点儿咖啡。

Sherry：谢谢。

默默：Sherry阿姨，你的眼睛真漂亮，是蓝色的。

Sherry：谢谢。

默默：你的头发也漂亮，是黄色的。

Sherry：谢谢。

默默：不过你的鼻子不好看，太大了。

Sherry：老外都是大鼻子。

[Wáng xiǎojiě jiā.]

Sherry: Nǐ hǎo a!

Mòmo: Nǐ hǎo!

Sherry: Nǐ jiào Mòmo, shì ma?

Mòmo: Shì a, nǐ ne, nǐ jiào shénme míngzi?

Sherry: Wǒ jiào Sherry, wǒ méiyǒu Zhōngguó míngzi.

Mòmo: Nǐ shì Měiguórén ma?

Sherry: Bú shì, wǒ shì Jiānádà rén.

Wáng xiǎojiě: Lái, hē diǎnr kāfēi.

Sherry: Xièxie.

Mòmo: Sherry āyí, nǐ de yǎnjing zhēn piàoliang, shì lánsè de.

Sherry: Xièxie.

Mòmo: Nǐ de tóufa yě piàoliang, shì huángsè de.

Sherry: Xièxie.

Mòmo: Búguò nǐ de bízi bù hǎokàn, tài dà le.

Sherry: Lǎowài dōu shì dà bízi.

注释 Notes

I

[*At Ms. Wang's home.*]

Sherry: How do you do?

Momo: How do you do?

Sherry: You are Momo, aren't you?

Momo: Yes, I am. What's your name?

Sherry: My name is Sherry and I don't have a Chinese name.

Momo: Are you American?

Sherry: No, I am Canadian.

Miss Wang: Would you like some coffee?

Sherry: Thanks.

Momo: Aunt Sherry, you have very beautiful blue eyes.

Sherry: Thank you.

Momo: Your blond hair is also beautiful.

Sherry: Thank you.

Momo: But your nose doesn't look beautiful. It's too big.

Sherry: Foreigners all have big noses.

① [你叫什么名字？] means "What's your name?", which is often used between peers or when a senior ask a junior. A more polite way of asking is "您贵姓？" Momo is still a child and is not aware of such social etiquette, so it is not considered offensive.

② In China, especially in small-and medium-sized cities or the countryside, many people do not meet foreigners very often, so when they see foreigners, they tend to ask all sorts of questions such as "What's your name?", "Where are you from?" and "What's your job?" In China it is acceptable to ask questions like this. They are not prying into your privacy and do not mean to be rude.

会话示例 Dialogues

II

[出租车里。]

司机：您好！您去哪儿？

乘客：去海淀图书大厦。

司机：好的。您是哪国人？②

乘客：我是英国人。

司机：你在中国做什么工作？

乘客：英语老师。

司机：那，工资很高吧。有多少啊？③

乘客：对不起，我听不懂。

司机：我问你的工资有多少。

乘客：不多，不多。

[Chūzūchē li.]

Sījī: Nín hǎo! Nín qù nǎr?

Chéngkè: Qù Hǎidiàn Túshū Dàshà.

Sījī: Hǎo de. Nín shì nǎ guó rén?

Chéngkè: Wǒ shì Yīngguórén.

Sījī: Nǐ zài Zhōngguó zuò shénme gōngzuò?

Chéngkè: Yīngyǔ lǎoshī.

Sījī: Nà, gōngzī hěn gāo ba, yǒu duōshao a?

Chéngkè: Duìbuqǐ, wǒ tīng bu dǒng.

Sījī: Wǒ wèn nǐ de gōngzī yǒu duōshao.

Chéngkè: Bù duō, bù duō.

注释 Notes

II

[*In a taxi.*]

Driver: Hello! Where are you going?

Passenger: Haidian Book Building.

Driver: OK . Which country are you from?

Passenger: I am from the UK.

Driver: What's your job in China?

Passenger: I am an English teacher.

Driver: Then, you must have a high salary. How much do you earn?

Passenger: Sorry, I don't understand.

Driver: I am asking how much you earn.

Passenger: Not much.

③ Until recently, Chinese salaries were connected to a person's rank, and were made public and transparent. The difference between salaries for different ranks was minimal, but if you had a high rank, you were accorded prestige and "face." No one minded questions about salary or the cost of something, since people made similar amount of money per month. Since the arrival of the market economy, the gap in salaries has widened considerably, and people, especially those at higher salary levels, do not like to talk about how much they make. People who are older or from the countryside may still ask you about your salary since they don't consider it being rude. You do not have to answer, of course, and you could tell them that "我们不习惯讲工资。Wǒmen bù xíguàn jiǎng gōngzī." , which means you are not accustomed to discussing salary. If your Chinese is not very good, you can also just act like you don't understand the question. The most important thing to remember is asking questions about money are not considered rude in China, and everything will go much better if you can overcome the feeling of being offended when you are asked about salary or money.

练习 Exercises

一、从右栏给左栏的词语找到相应的英文释义。

Match the Chinese words with the English ones.

名字	míngzi	nation
工作	gōngzuò	people; person
国	guó	salary
人	rén	name
工资	gōngzī	job

二、根据英文，把下面的词语连成一句话。

Make sentences with the given words.

1. Which country are you from?

____

哪 nǎ　是 shì　人 rén　国 guó　你 nǐ

2. What's your job?

____

做 zuò　你 nǐ　工作 gōngzuò　什么 shénme

三、根据你的实际情况回答问题。

Answer the questions accroding to your situation.

1. Q：你是哪国人？
   Nǐ shì nǎ guó rén?
   Which country are you from?
   A：__________________________

2. Q：你有中国名字吗？是什么？
   Nǐ yǒu Zhōngguó míngzi ma? Shì shénme?
   Do you have a Chinese name? What is it?
   A：__________________________

3. Q：你做什么工作？你喜欢你的工作吗？

Nǐ zuò shénme gōngzuò? Nǐ xǐhuan nǐ de gōngzuò ma?

What's your job? Do you like your job?

A：________________

四、实践汉语。

Practice your Chinese.

You're invited to a friend's home. Talk with other guests and make some new friends.

实用一点通 Cultural Tips

When you live or travel in China, you'll find some people asking questions such as "你是哪国人？(Where are you from?)" or "你的工资是多少？(How much is your monthly salary?)", but they are by no means invading your privacy. If you feel uncomfortable with any of the questions, you can leave them unanswered or pretend to be unable to understand them.

应变百宝囊 Language Enrichment

❶ 对不起，我听不懂。

Duìbuqǐ, wǒ tīng bu dǒng.

Sorry, I don't understand.

❷ 还行吧。

Hái xíng ba.

It's OK.

❸ 不多，不多。

Bù duō, bù duō.

Not much.

❹ 一般，一般。

Yìbān, yìbān.

Just so so.

❺ 日子过得还凑合。

Rìzi guò de hái còuhe.

Life isn't too bad.

❻ 日子马马虎虎过得去。

Rìzi mǎmǎhūhū guò de qù.

Life has been passable these days.

32 Lesson 32

谈天气

Tán Tiānqì

Talking about the Weather

学习主题 Subject

When you are travelling, you'll want to know what's the weather like in the destination. Where can you get this information? Weather also serves as a safe topic among friends. Find out here what you can say to them about weather.

学习重点 Language Focus

重点词 Key Words and Phrases

❶	天气	tiānqì	*n.*	weather
❷	度	dù	*m.*	*unit of measurement for temperature*
❸	热	rè	*adj.*	hot
❹	雨	yǔ	*n.*	rain
❺	下	xià	*v.*	(of rain, snow, etc.) fall
❻	雾	wù	*n.*	fog
❼	刮（风）	guā (fēng)	*v.*	(of the wind) blow

重点句 Key Sentences

❶ 明天天气怎么样?

Míngtiān tiānqì zěnmeyàng?

What will the weather be like tomorrow?

❷ 今天不冷也不热。

Jīntiān bù lěng yě bú rè.

It's neither cold nor hot today.

❸ 明天有大雨，会很冷。

Míngtiān yǒu dà yǔ, huì hěn lěng.

It will rain heavily tomorrow and will be very cold.

❹ 今天下雾了，雾还挺大的。

Jīntiān xià wù le, wù hái tǐng dà de.

It's foggy today, and the fog is quite heavy.

会话示例 Dialogues

I

A：今天天气真不错。

B：是啊。今天多少度？

A：二十五度①，很舒服。

B：是啊，不热也不冷，我想去爬山。

A：我也想去。

A: Jīntiān tiānqì zhēn búcuò.

B: Shì a, jīntiān duōshao dù?

A: Èrshíwǔ dù, hěn shūfu.

B: Shì a, bú rè yě bù lěng, wǒ xiǎng qù pá shān.

A: Wǒ yě xiǎng qù.

II

A：明天天气怎么样？

B：明天有大雨，会很冷。

A：明天很冷？

B：是啊，记着上课要带着伞啊②。

A: Míngtiān tiānqì zěnmeyàng?

B: Míngtiān yǒu dà yǔ, huì hěn lěng.

A: Míngtiān hěn lěng?

B: Shì a, jìzhe shàng kè yào dàizhe sǎn a.

III

A：早上好！

B：早上好啊。今天下雾了。

A：是啊，雾还挺大的，开车要很小心。

C：明天就好了，明天刮风。

D：而且还有大风。

A: Zǎoshang hǎo!

B: Zǎoshang hǎo a. Jīntiān xià wù le.

A: Shì a, wù hái tǐng dà de, kāi chē yào hěn xiǎoxīn.

C: Míngtiān jiù hǎo le, míngtiān guā fēng.

D: Érqiě hái yǒu dà fēng.

注释 Notes

I

A: It's nice today.

B: Yes, it is. What's the temperature today?

A: Twenty-five degrees, pretty comfortable.

B: Yes, neither hot nor cold. I feel like going climbing in the mountains.

A: So do I.

II

A: What will the weather be like tomorrow?

B: It's going to rain heavily and will be very cold.

A: Very cold?

B: Yes, remember to carry an umbrella to school.

III

A: Morning!

B: Morning! It is foggy today.

A: Yes, it is very foggy. You need to drive very carefully.

C: Tomorrow it will be better - it'll be windy.

D: It'll be gusty actually.

① Degrees here are in Celsius not in Fahrenheit. The freezing point of water is 0°C, or 32°F. And the boiling point is 100°C, or 212°F.

Some good markers are:

50°F is 10°C; 86°F is 30°C;

95°F is 35°C; 104°F is 40°C.

② When chatting with Chinese friends at the time of a sudden weather change, you'll find that after talking about the change, they'll remind you of how to cope with it. For instance, they'll tell you to put on more clothes when it is cold, carry an umbrella when it rains and walk carefully when it snows. Similar situations include telling friends to take care of their belongings and tickets when travelling. Chinese would be pleased to be reminded of such details and they will regard the person who does the reminding as considerate and caring. Generally speaking, the closer the relationship is, the more often the person will remind you of such details.

练习
Exercises

一、从右栏给左栏的词语找到相应的英文释义。
Match the Chinese words with the English ones.

天气	tiānqì	fog
雨	yǔ	cold
雾	wù	(of the wind) blow
冷	lěng	weather
刮风	guā fēng	rain

二、根据英文提示，用汉语说出下面的句子。
Make sentences with the given words.

1. It is neither cold nor hot today, and it's very comfortable.

   （冷lěng、热rè、舒服shūfu）

   ____

2. It'll be foggy tomorrow. Drive safely.

   （下雾xià wù、小心xiǎoxīn）

   ____

3. It will rain tomorrow. Remember to wear more clothes.

   （雨yǔ、衣服yīfu）

   ____

三、根据语境和提示词语，完成对话。

Complete the dialogues according to the given words or expressions and the context.

1. A：明天天气 ______________？（多少度 duōshao dù、怎么样 zěnmeyàng）

   Míngtiān tiānqì ______________?

   What will the weather be like tomorrow?

   B：明天下 ______________（风 fēng、雾 wù），还挺大的。

   Míngtiān xià ______________, hái tǐng dà de.

   Tomorrow it will... It'll be quite heavy.

2. A：星期六二十一度，______________。（冷 lěng、热 rè）

   Xīngqīliù èrshíyī dù, ______________.

   It'll be 21 degrees Celsius on Saturday. It's neither… nor….

   B：真不错，我们一起去爬山吧。

   Zhēn búcuò, wǒmen yìqǐ qù pá shān ba.

   Nice weather! Let's go climbing the mountains.

3. A：今天十一度，晚上还有雨。

   Jīntiān shíyī dù, wǎnshang hái yǒu yǔ.

   It's 11 degrees Celsius today and will rain tonight.

   B：是 ______________ 冷的(挺 tǐng、太 tài)，多穿些衣服吧。

   Shì ______________ lěng de, duō chuān xiē yīfu ba.

   It's rather…. Dress warmly.

   A：嗯，你也一样。

   En, nǐ yě yíyàng.

   The same to you.

四、实践汉语。

Practice your Chinese.

Your parents are coming to China to visit you. Tell them what the weather is like in your city recently and suggest what kinds of clothes they need to take.

实用一点通 Cultural Tips

To know the weather of your destination is important for a traveler, but the broadcaster speaks too fast for you to keep up with the forecast in both TV and radio. What shall you do? A useful tip is to remember this sentence “明天天气怎么样？” (How’s the weather tomorrow?). You can ask your friends and get the answer. Please note that degree Celsius instead of Fahrenheit is generally used here.

城市天气预报常用的天气符号

应变百宝囊 Language Enrichment

❶	阴	yīn	overcast
❷	晴转阴	qíng zhuǎn yīn	sunny to overcast
❸	晴	qíng	fine; clear
❹	雨夹雪	yǔ jiā xuě	sleet; rain mixed with snow
❺	雪	xuě	snow
❻	小到中雨	xiǎo dào zhōng yǔ	light to moderate rain
❼	多云	duōyún	cloudy
❽	最高气温	zuì gāo qìwēn	the highest temperature
❾	最低气温	zuì dī qìwēn	the lowest temperature
❿	干燥	gānzào	dry
⓫	风沙	fēngshā	sand blown by wind
⓬	湿润	shīrùn	wet
⓭	降温	jiàng wēn	a drop of temperature
⓮	台风	táifēng	typhoon
⓯	大风	dà fēng	gust

33 Lesson 33

赠送礼物

Zèngsòng Lǐwù

Giving Presents

学习主题 Subject

Gifts are important for Chinese, for they take gifts as an effective way to express their inner feelings toward others. That's why you should know some do's and don'ts about gift-giving as well as some useful oral expressions.

学习重点 Language Focus

重点词 Key Words and Phrases

1	给	gěi	*v.*	give
2	礼物	lǐwù	*n.*	gift; present
3	不好意思	bù hǎoyìsi	*IE.*	feel embarrassed
4	太	tài	*adv.*	too
5	客气	kèqi	*adj.*	polite
6	代	dài	*prep.*	on one's behalf
7	心意	xīnyì	*n.*	regards, kind feeling

重点句 Key Sentences

1. 这是给你的礼物。
   Zhè shì gěi nǐ de lǐwù.
   Here's a present for you.

2. 拿着吧，这是我们的心意。
   Názhe ba, zhè shì wǒmen de xīnyì.
   Please accept it. It shows our appreciation.

3. 不好意思，你太客气了。
   Bù hǎoyìsi, nǐ tài kèqi le.
   It's very kind of you.

4. 我代她谢谢你。
   Wǒ dài tā xièxie nǐ.
   I'd like to thank you on her behalf.

会话示例 Dialogues

I

[家里。]

客人：对了①，哥哥，这是给你的礼物。

主人：谢谢，不好意思，你太客气了。

客人：小妹在哪儿呢？这是给她的礼物。

主人：我代她谢谢你了。

客人：不客气。

[Jiāli.]

Kèrén: Duìle, gēge, zhè shì gěi nǐ de lǐwù.

Zhǔrén: Xièxie, bù hǎoyìsi, nǐ tài kèqi le.

Kèrén: Xiǎo mèi zài nǎr ne? Zhè shì gěi tā de lǐwù.

Zhǔrén: Wǒ dài tā xièxie nǐ le.

Kèrén: Bú kèqi.

II

[马路上。]

A：给，小王！

小王：我不要，王太太。

A：吃吧，不要客气。

小王：我真的不要，谢谢。

A：吃吧，吃吧，很好吃。

小王：不，不……

B：您别客气，吃吧。

小王：好的，好的，谢谢您！

[Mǎlù shang.]

A: Gěi, Xiǎo Wáng!

Xiǎo Wáng: Wǒ bú yào, Wáng tàitai.

A: Chī ba, bú yào kèqi.

Xiǎo Wáng: Wǒ zhēn de bú yào, xièxie.

A: Chī ba, chī ba, hěn hǎochī.

Xiǎo Wáng: Bù, bù……

B: Nín bié kèqi, chī ba.

Xiǎo Wáng: Hǎo de, hǎo de, xièxie nín!

注释 Notes

I

[*At home.*]

Guest: Oh, right, Brother, here's a present for you.

Host: Thank you so much!

Guest: Where is Little Sister? I have a present for her.

Host: Thanks on her behalf.

Guest: You are welcome.

II

[*In the street.*]

A: Xiao Wang, here you are.

Xiao Wang:

No, thanks, Mrs. Wang.

A: Come on, have some. Don't be shy.

Xiao Wang:

No, thanks.

A: Have some. It's really good.

Xiao Wang:

No...

B: No need to be shy. Have some.

Xiao Wang:

OK, thank you.

① In the context, "对了" doesn't mean "correct". It is used when you suddenly think of something. A bit like the English "Oh!".

会话示例 Dialogues

Ⅲ

男士：王小姐，很高兴认识你，谢谢你这些天陪我们游览北京。

Nánshì: Wáng xiǎojiě, hěn gāoxìng rènshi nǐ, xièxie nǐ zhè xiē tiān péi wǒmen yóulǎn Běijīng.

王小姐：我和你们在一起也很高兴。

Wáng xiǎojiě: Wǒ hé nǐmen zài yìqǐ yě hěn gāoxìng.

Sherry：王小姐，明天我们就要回美国了。这个是我们的一点儿心意。

Sherry: Wáng xiǎojiě, míngtiān wǒmen jiù yào huí Měiguó le. Zhège shì wǒmen de yìdiǎnr xīnyì.

王小姐：不，不，你们太客气了。②

Wáng xiǎojiě: Bù, bù, nǐmen tài kèqi le.

Sherry：拿着吧，这是我们的心意。这次旅游我们很高兴，很满意。

Sherry: Názhe ba, zhè shì wǒmen de xīnyì. Zhè cì lǚyóu wǒmen hěn gāoxìng, hěn mǎnyì.

男士：拿着吧。

Nánshì: Názhe ba.

王小姐：那，那好吧，谢谢你们。

Wáng xiǎojiě: Nà, nà hǎo ba, xièxie nǐmen.

Sherry：不要客气。

Sherry: Búyào kèqi.

注释 Notes

III

Man: Ms. Wang, nice meeting you. Thank you for guiding us through Beijing over the past few days.

Ms. Wang:

I am happy to be with you.

Sherry:

Ms. Wang, we are going back to the US tomorrow. This is to show our appreciation.

Ms. Wang:

No, thank you.

Sherry:

Please accept it. It shows our appreciation. We are very happy with the trip.

Man: Please take it.

Ms. Wang:

Alright, then I'll take it. Thanks.

Sherry:

You are welcome.

② In China, when you offer presents to your friends, or even just something to eat or drink on a trip, their first reaction is almost always "No, thank you." But if you offer several times, it is likely that they will accept it. Apart from "你太客气了" (It's very kind of you), you may also hear "不好意思" (I do not deserve this or I am embarrassed to accept this.) If one is giving a person some money, it is common that he/she will slip it into the person's pocket.

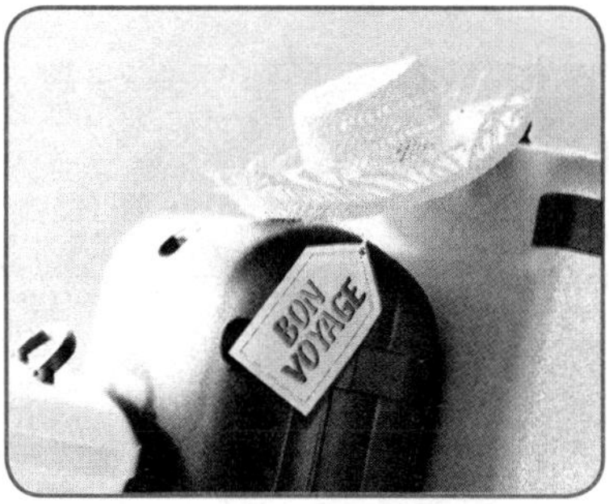

练习 Exercises

一、从右栏给左栏的词语找到相应的英文释义。

Match the Chinese expressions with the English ones.

给	gěi	on one's behalf
礼物	lǐwù	regards, kind feeling
代	dài	take
心意	xīnyì	give
拿	ná	gift; present

二、意念表达。

Express the following functions and notions.

1. Your landlord is very kind to you. Offer him a gift when you move out.
2. You accept a gift on your sister's behalf. Thank the person who gives her the gift.

三、根据语境，完成对话。

Complete the dialogues according to the context.

1. A：____________________

   B：你太客气了。

   Nǐ tài kèqi le.

   It's very kind of you.

2. A：____________________

   B：和你们在一起我也很高兴。

   Hé nǐmen zài yìqǐ wǒ yě hěn gāoxìng.

   I'm happy to be with you too.

四、实践汉语。

Practice your Chinese.

Your Chinese friend is having a birthday party. And you will go with your child.

实用一点通
Cultural Tips

Chinese believe in "courtesy demands reciprocity" and when one gives a gift to others, he/she will generally expect a present in return. Therefore, when you receive a gift from a Chinese friend, be sure to remember to choose an appropriate time and present a gift in return. This will give your friend a good impression of being polite and emphasizing the friendship between you two. The gift given in return has almost the same value as the one you have received. It should be something your friend will like or in need of.

应变百宝囊
Language Enrichment

❶	盒子	hézi	box
❷	首饰	shǒushì	jewelry
❸	包装纸	bāozhuāngzhǐ	wrapping paper
❹	饰品	shìpǐn	accessory
❺	红包	hóngbāo	red envelope containing money
❻	玩具	wánjù	toy
❼	贵重	guìzhòng	expensive
❽	鲜花	xiānhuā	flower
❾	高档	gāodàng	top grade
❿	蛋糕	dàngāo	cake

34
Lesson 34

告辞

Gàocí

Bidding Farewell

学习主题
Subject

After you dine at a friend's house and are about to leave, what should you say? If you have to go before a happy get-together comes to an end, what should you say?

学习重点 Language Focus

重点词 Key Words and Phrases

❶	辛苦	xīnkǔ	*v.*	toil
❷	早	zǎo	*adj.*	early
❸	该……了	gāi……le	*IE.*	It's time...
❹	走	zǒu	*v.*	leave
❺	休息	xiūxi	*v.*	have a rest
❻	先	xiān	*adv.*	earlier
❼	忙	máng	*adj.*	busy

重点句 Key Sentences

❶ 不早了，该走了。

Bù zǎo le, gāi zǒu le.

It's late and I should go.

❷ 辛苦您了。

Xīnkǔ nín le.

I'm sorry to trouble you.

❸ 你先忙/休息吧，我走了。

Nǐ xiān máng/xiūxi ba, wǒ zǒu le.

I'm leaving. Please go back to your work/have a rest.

会话示例 Dialogues

I

客人A：阿姨，您做的菜挺好吃的。

主人A：那有时间常来吃饭吧。①

客人们：好啊！②

客人B：阿姨，辛苦您了。

主人A：没什么。③

客人A：不早了，我们该走了。

客人B：是啊。

主人B：不再坐会儿了？

客人B：不了，你们休息吧，我们走了。

Kèrén A: Āyí, nín zuò de cài tǐng hǎochī de.

Zhǔrén A: Nà yǒu shíjiān cháng lái chī fàn ba.

Kèrén men: Hǎo a!

Kèrén B: Āyí, xīnkǔ nín le.

Zhǔrén A: Méi shénme.

Kèrén A: Bù zǎo le, wǒmen gāi zǒu le.

Kèrén B: Shì a.

Zhǔrén B: Bú zài zuò huìr le?

Kèrén B: Bù le, nǐmen xiūxi ba, wǒmen zǒu le.

II

A：您看，时间不早了，我还有事儿，我先走了。④

B：哦。

A：您先忙吧，我走了。

A: Nín kàn, shíjiān bù zǎo le, wǒ hái yǒu shìr, wǒ xiān zǒu le.

B: Ò.

A: Nín xiān máng ba, wǒ zǒu le.

注释 Notes

I

Guest A: Aunty, you are a really good cook.

Host A: Come to have dinner with us more often then.

Guests: We'd love to!

Guest B: Aunty, thank you for all the trouble.

Host A: It's nothing.

Guest A: It's getting late. We've got to go.

Guest B: Yes.

Host B: Wouldn't you stay a little longer?

Guest B: No, thank you. You please take a rest, and we are leaving.

II

A: It's late. I've got something to do, and I have to go now.

B: OK.

A: Surc, scc you.

① Although many people would take their friends out to dinner, some prefer to eat at home with close friends, as it is more relaxing and homey. In particular, parents welcome friends of their children to eat at home.

② In China, how people are treated depends on how close they are. The closer the relationship, the fewer the formalities and thus the more natural the atmosphere. In the dialogue, when the hostess invites the guests to come to dinner more often, they respond with "好啊" (We'd love to)" instead of "这太麻烦你了" (It's too much bother)" or "真不好意思" (Sorry to bother you)". From this we can tell that they must be very close to the children of the aunt and must have been frequent visitors to the home. Given such relationship, if you act too formal it will upset the host who may feel you are keeping too much of a distance.

③ [没什么] means "It doesn't matter" or "You're welcome", which is similar to "没关系" or "没事儿". When you receive thanks or compliments, you may also respond by saying "没什么". The two guests readily accept the invitation of the aunt to come more often and

注释 Notes

show their thanks. B says "辛苦您了" (Thanks for all the trouble), to which the aunt responds with "没什么".

④ [我还有事，我先走了] means that "I've got something to do and I have to go now", which is often used when Chinese say goodbye. You may be wondering what this "something" means since it is very vague. This is just a way to politely refuse an invitation. If you don't want to attend a party, and if you give excuses, sometimes the Chinese might find your reason not to be a good one, so you might as well just respond by saying "我还有事儿。wǒ hái yǒu shìr." In the West, specifics are given ("I have an appointment" or "I have to work late") and are considered good reasons for declining an invitation, but in China it is polite to not be specific and just say "我有事儿。wǒ yǒu shìr.".

练习
Exercises

一、从右栏给左栏的词语找到相应的英文释义。

Match the Chinese expressions with the English ones.

辛苦	xīnkǔ	busy
走	zǒu	earlier
休息	xiūxi	toil
忙	máng	have a rest
先	xiān	leave

二、意念表达。

Express the following functions and notions.

1. Invite your friends to come to your home more often.
2. Properly end your talk with someone.

三、选择合适的选项完成对话。

Choose the proper answer to complete the dialogue.

A. 辛苦您了。
Xīnkǔ nín le.
Thanks for all the trouble.

B. 没什么。
Méi shénme.
You're welcome.

C. 有时间常来。
Yǒu shíjiān cháng lái.
Come more often when you have time.

D. 不了，你们休息吧。
Bù le, nǐmen xiūxi ba.
No, thanks. You please take a rest.

1. A：______________

B：不客气。

Bú kèqi.

You're welcome.

2. A：不早了，你们休息吧。

Bù zǎo le, nǐmen xiūxi ba.

It's getting late. You please take a rest.

B：______________

3. A：谢谢您的帮助。

Xièxie nín de bāngzhù.

Thanks for your help.

B：______________

四、实践汉语。

Practice your Chinese.

After visiting a friend in a hospital, how do you say goodbye'to him/her?

实用一点通
Cultural Tips

When you visit a Chinere friend and it's time for you to say goodbye, he/she will ask you to stay, which is a same way to show hospitality and politeness as they say "you shouldn't have done that" when you present them a gift. If it's really late or you really have to go, just say so and they'll let you go, for they just want to show their hospitality.

应变百宝囊
Language Enrichment

❶ 我还要办点儿事，告辞了。
Wǒ hái yào bàn diǎnr shì, gàocí le.
I have something to do. Bye!

❷ 时间不早了，我得走了。
Shíjiān bù zǎo le, wǒ děi zǒu le.
It's getting late. I've got to go.

❸ 对不起，不能奉陪了。
Duìbuqǐ, bù néng fèngpéi le.
Sorry, I have to go.

❹ 我还得上班，失陪了。
Wǒ hái děi shàng bān, shīpéi le.
Excuse me, I have to go to work.

❺ 不远送了，欢迎再来。
Bù yuǎn sòng le, huānyíng zài lái.
Goodbye. Come again.

❻ 有时间来玩儿吧。
Yǒu shíjiān lái wánr ba.
Come again when you have time.

❼ 有空儿常来坐坐。
Yǒu kòngr cháng lái zuòzuo.
Come to visit us when you have time.

❽ 再见！您走好！
Zàijiàn! Nín zǒu hǎo!
Bye. Take care.

35 Lesson 35

委婉地拒绝

Wěiwǎn de Jùjué

Refusing an Invitation

学习主题 Subject

To say NO is sometimes a must but will also cause unease. Learn the best way to say no here from native Chinese.

学习重点 Language Focus

重点词 Key Words and Phrases

❶ 事（情）	shì (qing)	*n.*	thing
❷ 巧	qiǎo	*adj.*	coincidental
❸ 改天	gǎi tiān	*n.*	sometime later; another day
❹ 能	néng	*v.*	can; be able to
❺ 但是	dànshì	*conj.*	but
❻ 有（一）点儿	yǒu (yì) diǎnr	*adv.*	a little; a bit
❼ 下（一）次	xià (yí) cì	*n.*	next time

重点句 Key Sentences

❶ 我家里有事。

Wǒ jiāli yǒu shì.

I have something to do with my family.

❷ 改天吧。

Gǎi tiān ba.

Let's do it another day.

❸ 下（一）次吧。

Xià (yí) cì ba.

Maybe next time.

❹ 太不巧了。

Tài bù qiǎo le.

What a pity!

❺ 我现在有点儿忙，不能去。

Wǒ xiànzài yǒudiǎnr máng, bù néng qù.

I'm a little busy now, so I can't go.

会话示例 Dialogues

I

A：一起去打球吧。

B：不好意思，我今天有事。

A：哟，太不巧了。①那，改天吧。

A: Yìqǐ qù dǎ qiú ba.

B: Bù hǎoyìsi, wǒ jīntiān yǒu shì.

A: Yō, tài bù qiǎo le. Nà, gǎi tiān ba.

II

A：许畅，我的电脑坏了。你能来帮我修修吗？

B：好啊，但是我现在有点儿忙。下午好吗？

A：好的，好的，谢谢你。

B：那下午见。

A: Xǔ Chàng, wǒ de diànnǎo huài le. Nǐ néng lái bāng wǒ xiūxiu ma?

B: Hǎo a, dànshì wǒ xiànzài yǒudiǎnr máng. Xiàwǔ hǎo ma?

A: Hǎo de, hǎo de, xièxie nǐ.

B: Nà xiàwǔ jiàn.

III

A：你帮我修好了电脑，我得好好儿谢谢你。

B：不用客气。今天，我家里有点儿事，不能在这儿吃饭，下次吧。②

A: Nǐ bāng wǒ xiūhǎole diànnǎo, wǒ děi hǎohāor xièxie nǐ.

B: Bú yòng kèqi. Jīntiān, wǒ jiāli yǒudiǎnr shì, bù néng zài zhèr chī fàn, xià cì ba.

注释 Notes

I

A: Let's go to play ball.

B: Sorry, I am engaged today.

A: Really? That's too bad! Maybe some other day.

II

A: Xu Chang , my computer is down. Could you help me fix it?

B: OK, but I am busy now. How about this afternoon?

A: Sure, thanks.

B: Then, see you this afternoon.

III

A: Thank you for fixing the computer for me. How about having dinner together?

B: You are welcome. I have something to do and can't make it today. Maybe next time, OK?

① In China, when someone extends an invitation and you can't make it or you have to decline, do not respond with "不" or "不行". Instead, you may decline with "太不巧了！(What a pity!)" or "我今天有事(I'm engaged today.)" followed by "改天吧(Let's do it another day)" or "下次吧(Maybe next time)". You can also reschedule the event.

② [上] means "last" or "previous", indicating an earlier time and prior order. For instance, "上星期一" means "last Monday". The opposite of "上" is "下", meaning "next" or "following". For instance, "下星期五(next Friday)".

练习 Exercises

一、从右栏给左栏的词语找到相应的英文释义。

Match the Chinese expressions with the English ones.

下次	xià cì	now
一起	yìqǐ	busy
吃饭	chī fàn	a little
现在	xiànzài	next time
忙	máng	together
有点儿	yǒudiǎnr	have a meal

二、意念表达。

Express the following functions and notions.

1. A friend invites you to dinner this evening, but you can't make it. Reschedule it for tomorrow evening.
2. A friend asks if you can go climbing with him/her, but you can't make it.

三、选择合适的选项完成对话。

Choose the proper answer to complete the dialogue.

A. 不好意思。
Bù hǎoyìsi.
Sorry.

B. 太不巧了。
Tài bù qiǎo le.
What a pity!

C. 不用客气。
Bú yòng kèqi.
Please don't stand on ceremony.

D. 可以。
Kěyǐ.
Sure.

E. 哪里，哪里。
Nǎli, nǎli.
Thanks.

F. 那好吧。
Nà hǎo ba.
OK.

1. A：这是我们的一点儿心意，拿着吧。

Zhè shì wǒmen de yìdiǎnr xīnyì, názhe ba.

Here's a gift to show our appreciation. Please accept it.

B：__________，你太客气了。

__________, nǐ tài kèqi le.

..., you are being too polite.

2. A：晚上我们一起吃饭吧。

Wǎnshang wǒmen yìqǐ chī fàn ba.

Let's have dinner together.

B：__________，今天晚上我家里有事。

__________, jīntiān wǎnshang wǒ jiāli yǒu shì.

..., I have something to do with my family this evening.

3. A：七点在电影院门口见面，好吗？

Qī diǎn zài diànyǐngyuàn ménkǒu jiàn miàn, hǎo ma?

Shall we meet at the movie theater at seven?

B：__________，七点我在电影院门口等你。

__________, qī diǎn wǒ zài diànyǐngyuàn ménkǒu děng nǐ.

..., see you then.

四、实践汉语。

Practice your Chinese.

A close friend of yours is getting married, but you can't attend the wedding ceremony. Explain to your friend.

实用一点通 Cultural Tips

When you turn down an invitation for an appointment, you can say "我有事" (I have something else to do) instead of providing detailed explanation. But a friend might insist after your refusal and even ask you to cancel your original arrangement. Please don't be upset and you can stick to you plan by saying "我真的有事" (I really have other things to do) and your friend will let you go.

应变百宝囊
Language Enrichment

❶ 考虑考虑再说吧。

Kǎolǜ kǎolǜ zài shuō ba.

Let me think about it.

❷ 再等等吧。

Zài děngdeng ba.

Give me some time.

❸ 有点儿难办。

Yǒudiǎnr nán bàn.

It is kind of difficult.

❹ 对不起，可能办不到。

Duìbuqǐ, kěnéng bàn bú dào.

Sorry, I am afraid that I can't help.

❺ 我最近实在太忙。

Wǒ zuìjìn shízài tài máng.

I have been very busy lately.

❻ 我已经有约会了，实在抱歉。

Wǒ yǐjīng yǒu yuēhuì le, shízài bàoqiàn.

I already have an appointment. I'm sorry.

❼ 过两天我再找你吧。

Guò liǎng tiān wǒ zài zhǎo nǐ ba.

I will talk to you in a couple of days, okay?

❽ 我们再研究研究。

Wǒmen zài yánjiū yánjiū.

We'll discuss it later.

36 Lesson 36

情绪的表达

Qíngxù de Biǎodá

Complaining

学习主题 Subject

Here you will learn how to react appropriately when encountering unhappy and unfavorable situations.

学习重点 Language Focus

重点词 Key Words and Phrases

1	渴	kě	*adj.*	thirsty
2	死	sǐ	*adj.*	dead
3	怎么	zěnme	*qp.*	why
4	生气	shēng qì	*adj.*	angry
5	着急	zháo jí	*adj.*	anxious
6	碰	pèng	*v.*	touch

重点句 Key Sentences

1. 我有点儿渴了。
   Wǒ yǒudiǎnr kě le.
   I'm a little thirsty.

2. 那怎么办?
   Nà zěnme bàn?
   What shall we do then?

3. 怎么可以这样呢!
   Zěnme kěyǐ zhèyàng ne?
   How could this be!

4. 渴死了。
   Kěsǐ le.
   I'm extremely thirsty.

5. 不要碰我。
   Bú yào pèng wǒ.
   Don't touch me.

6. 不要生气/着急。
   Bú yào shēng qì/zháo jí.
   Don't be angry/be anxious.

会话示例 Dialogues

I

A: 怎么啦？
B: 我有点儿渴。
A: 再休息会儿吧，一会儿去买喝的①。
B: 走吧，走吧，我渴死②啦。
A: 好，好，好。

A: Zěnme la?
B: Wǒ yǒudiǎnr kě.
A: Zài xiūxi huìr ba, yíhuìr qù mǎi hē de.
B: Zǒu ba, zǒu ba, wǒ kěsǐ la.
A: Hǎo, hǎo, hǎo.

II

White：车怎么③还没有来？
White夫人：不是说好了八点半吗？
王小姐：是啊，现在都九点了。
White：怎么可以这样呢！
王小姐：不要生气。
White：那怎么办？
王小姐：不要着急，你们先回房间，我再联系一辆出租车吧。
White：好吧。

White: Chē zěnme hái méiyǒu lái?
White fūrén: Bú shì shuōhǎole bā diǎn bàn ma?
Wáng xiǎojiě: Shì a, xiànzài dōu jiǔ diǎn le.
White: Zěnme kěyǐ zhèyàng ne!
Wáng xiǎojiě: Bú yào shēng qì.
White: Nà zěnme bàn?
Wáng xiǎojiě: Bú yào zháo jí, nǐmen xiān huí fángjiān, wǒ zài liánxì yí liàng chūzūchē ba.
White: Hǎo ba.

注释 Notes

I

A: What's wrong?

B: I am a little thirsty.

A: Take more rest. I'll get something to drink later.

B: Come on, let's go. I am dying for a drink.

A: All right.

II

Mr. White: Why hasn't the car arrived?

Mrs. White: Didn't we agree on eight thirty?

Ms. Wang: Yes, it is already nine.

Mr. White: How could this be!

Ms. Wang: Don't get angry.

Mr. White: What are we supposed to do now?

Ms. Wang: Don't worry. Could you go back to your room to wait, and I'll try to get a cab?

Mr. White: OK.

① [喝的] refers to "something to drink". "v.+的" or "vp.+的" is a pattern of "的" phrases, such as "买两张到上海的（到上海的票）", which means "Can I have two tickets to Shanghai?"

② [渴] means "thirsty" and "死" means "die" and they are used here just to indicate that she is extremely thirsty. In general, Chinese people don't like to talk about death, and they tend to exaggerate, so using the expression "thirsty to death" is an extreme case. But with close friends, we may express our feelings without any reservation. If you are really thirsty, you may also say to your friends that "我渴死啦", or you may say "我太渴了". "adj.+死了" is just an indication of the extreme degree of the adj. used to show a bad feeling, such as "累死了(extremely tired)" and "冷死了(extremely cold)".

会话示例 Dialogues

III

小女孩儿：

叔叔好。

同学A：好，好。

同学B：好久不见啦，老同学。

同学C：是啊。

[同学B喜爱地捏了一下孩子的脸蛋儿。]

同学B：真可爱！

小女孩儿：

请不要碰我。④

[同学们笑起来。]

同学B：小姑娘长大了啊。

Xiǎo nǚháir: Shūshu hǎo.

Tóngxué A: Hǎo, hǎo.

Tóngxué B: Hǎo jiǔ bú jiàn la, lǎo tóngxué.

Tóngxué C: Shì a.

[Tóngxué B xǐ'ài de niēle yíxià háizi de liǎndànr.]

Tóngxué B: Zhēn kě'ài!

Xiǎo nǚháir: Qǐng bú yào pèng wǒ.

[Tóngxuémen xiào qǐlai.]

Tóngxué B: Xiǎo gūniang zhǎng dàle a.

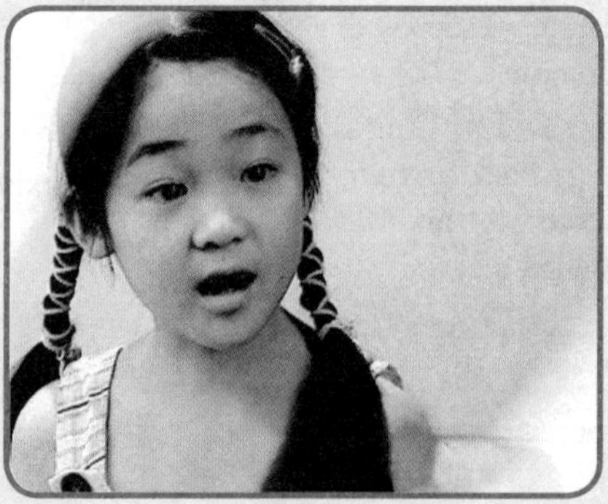

注释 Notes

III

Girl: Nice to meet you, Uncle.

Classmate A:
Nice to meet you too.
Classmate B:
Haven't seen you for quite a long time!
Classmate C: Yes.

[***Classmate B pinches the face of the girl.***]
Classmate B:
A lovely girl.
Girl: Please don't touch me.

[*The crowd bursts into laughter.*]
Classmate B:
The little girl has grown up.

③ [怎么] can be used to inquire about reasons. For instance, "你怎么生气了？" means "Why are you mad?" It can also be used to inquire the actions to take. For instance,

我们该怎么办？

Wǎmen gāi zěnme bàn?

What are we supposed to do?

④ In China, adults often touch the head or face of children out of affection. If you don't like this, you may respond by saying "请不要碰我 (Please don't touch me)".

练习 Exercises

一、从右栏给左栏的词语找到相应的英文释义。

Match the Chinese words with the English ones.

累	lèi	go
碰	pèng	dead
去	qù	buy
死	sǐ	touch
买	mǎi	tired

二、意念表达。

Express the following functions and notions.

1. It's freezing, and finally the friend you're waiting for arrives. Complain to him/her about his/her being late.
2. You friend likes giving you a pat on the shoulder, but now your shoulders hurt. Tell him/her not to do so.

三、根据语境，完成对话。

Complete the dialogues according to the context.

1. A：小王，________________。

   Xiǎo Wáng, ________________.

   Xiao Wang, … .

   B：那，我们休息一会儿吧。

   Nà, wǒmen xiūxi yíhuìr ba.

   Let's take a rest then.

   A：________________，你呢？

   ________________, nǐ ne?

   ..., what about you?

   B：我也有点儿渴，我们去买点儿喝的吧。

   Wǒ yě yǒudiǎnr kě, wǒmen qù mǎi diǎnr hē de ba.

   I'm a little thirsty too. Let's get something to drink.

2. A：小王说他不能来了。
Xiǎo Wáng shuō tā bù néng lái le.
Xiao Wang said he couldn't come.
B：＿＿＿＿＿＿＿＿，他自己说他一定来的。
＿＿＿＿＿＿＿＿，tā zìjǐ shuō tā yídìng lái de.
..., He said he definitely would come.
A：但是他也不想生病啊。
Dànshì tā yě bù xiǎng shēng bìng a.
But surely he didn't want to fall ill.
B：不好意思，我不知道他生病了。
Bù hǎoyìsi, wǒ bù zhīdào tā shēng bìng le.
Sorry, I didn't know he was sick.

四、实践汉语。
Practice your Chinese.

Suppose you seem to be especially unlucky today - first you were held up in a traffic jam, then you lost your wallet/purse. Talk with your friends.

实用一点通
Cultural Tips

Generally, a Chinese would lose temper in two situations. One is where there are all strangers, and a quarrel might break out due to a trivial incident; and the other one is in front of families and friends, for there is no need to hide one's real feeling here. But the reaction you get could be quite different. When you lose temper with strangers, they would fight back at once; but when it comes to your close friends, they might tolerate your bad temper.

应变百宝囊
Language Enrichment

❶ 困	kùn	drowsy
❷ 郁闷	yùmèn	gloomy
❸ 麻烦	máfan	troublesome
❹ 倒霉	dǎo méi	have bad luck
❺ 烦	fán	be tired of
❻ 脏	zāng	dirty
❼ 担心	dān xīn	be worried

37
Lesson 37

爱意的表达

Àiyì de Biǎodá

Expressing Love

学习主题
Subject

Fall in love with a Chinese? If you can't find ways to tell him/her directly, here's how to let him/her know and finally accept your love.

学习重点 Language Focus

重点词 Key Words and Phrases

❶	花	huā	*n.*	flower
❷	多	duō	*adv.*	to a great extent
❸	漂亮	piàoliang	*adj.*	beautiful
❹	好	hǎo	*adv.*	very; quite
❺	真	zhēn	*adv.*	really
❻	眼睛	yǎnjing	*n.*	eye
❼	喜欢	xǐhuan	*v.*	like

重点句 Key Sentences

❶ 我喜欢你。

Wo xǐhuan nǐ.

I like you.

❷ 我喜欢你的眼睛。

Wǒ xǐhuan nǐ de yǎnjing.

I like your eyes.

❸ 你比花更漂亮。

Nǐ bǐ huā gèng piàoliang.

You're more beautiful than flowers.

❹ 多漂亮啊！

Duō piàoliang a!

How beautiful it is!

会话示例 Dialogues

I

[男孩儿和女孩儿漫步在公园里。]

男孩儿：你看，这花多①漂亮。

女孩儿：是啊，好漂亮啊。

男孩儿：真漂亮啊！

女孩儿：说什么呢！

男孩儿：真的，你比花更漂亮。② 特别是你的眼睛。我喜欢你的眼睛。

[女孩儿害羞地走开。]

女孩儿：看，那边儿的花也开了。

[Nánháir hé nǚháir mànbù zài gōngyuán li.]

Nánháir: Nǐ kàn, zhè huā duō piàoliang.

Nǚháir: Shì a, hǎo piàoliang a.

Nánháir: Zhēn piàoliang a!

Nǚháir: Shuō shénme ne!

Nánháir: Zhēn de, nǐ bǐ huā gèng piàoliang. Tèbié shì nǐ de yǎnjing. Wǒ xǐhuan nǐ de yǎnjing.

[Nǚháir hài xiū de zǒukāi.]

Nǚháir: Kàn, nàbiānr de huā yě kāi le.

注释 Notes

I

[*A boy and a girl take a stroll in a park.*]

Boy: Look at this. Isn't the flower beautiful?

Girl: Yes, it is!

Boy: It is just so beautiful.

Girl: What are you talking about?

Boy: Yes, you are more beautiful than the flowers. Especially your eyes. I like your eyes.

[*The girl walks away bashfully.*]

Girl: Look, there are flowers blooming over there.

① [多] means "many", but in this context, "多" means "very". "多" is often used in phrases of "多+adj." to indicate a higher degree or stronger emotion. For instance,

A：看，这孩子多可爱啊！
Kàn, zhè háizi duō kě'ài a!
Look, how lovely the child is!
B：是啊，真的很可爱。
Shì a, zhēn de hěn kě'ài.
Yes, she (he) is really lovely.

② Chinese tend to be indirect. Note the comparison in this case, where the girl and a flower is being compared. Saying the girl is more beautiful than a flower is an euphemistic way of complimenting the girl for her beauty. You may also compliment girls around you in such a way. "比" is used to construct the comparsion in the structure "A+比+B+adj.". For instance,

北京比上海干燥。
Běijīng bǐ Shànghǎi gānzào.
Beijing is drier than Shanghai.

会话示例 Dialogues

Ⅱ

[两人休息后起身。]

男孩儿：我送你回家吧。

女孩儿：不用啦。

男孩儿：有时间再一起看电影，好吗？

女孩儿：好吧，打电话吧。我先走啦！

[男孩儿叫住女孩儿。]

男孩儿：璐璐，等一下。

女孩儿：什么事？

男孩儿：璐璐，我喜欢你。璐璐，再见！

[说完，幸福地跑了。]

[Liǎng rén xiūxi hòu qǐ shēn.]

Nánháir: Wǒ sòng nǐ huí jiā ba.

Nǚháir: Bú yòng la.

Nánháir: Yǒu shíjiān zài yìqǐ kàn diànyǐng, hǎo ma?

Nǚháir: Hǎo ba, dǎ diànhuà ba. Wǒ xiān zǒu la!

[nánháir jiàozhù nǚháir.]

Nánháir: Lùlu, děng yíxià.

Nǚháir: Shénme shì?

Nánháir: Lùlu, wǒ xǐhuan nǐ. Lùlu, zàijiàn!

[Shuōwán, xìngfú de pǎo le.]

注释 Notes

II

[*The two stand up after a rest.*]

Boy: Let me take you home.

Girl: No, thanks.

Boy: Let's go to a movie next time, shall we?

Girl: Ok, just call me. Bye!

[*The boy asks the girl to stop.*]

Boy: Lulu, just wait a minute.

Girl: What's up?

Boy: Lulu, I love you. Bye, Lulu!

[*Having said that, the boy runs away happily.*]

练习 Exercises

一、从右栏给左栏的词语找到相应的英文释义。

Match the Chinese words with the English ones.

好吃	hǎochī	like
漂亮	piàoliang	satisfied
喜欢	xǐhuan	passable
满意	mǎnyì	beautiful
可以	kěyǐ	delicious

二、意念表达。

Express the following functions and notions.

1. Compliment a good friend.
2. Your neighbor has a lovely kid. Praise her / him.

三、看看遇到下面的情景你该怎么说。

Fill in the blanks according to the context.

Suppose you are around twenty.

If you fall in love with a Chinese girl, you can say

____

If today is one of your female colleagues' birthday, you can say

____

If you are invited to a Chinese friend's home and see his/her child, you can say

____

If your friend helps you fix your computer, you can say

____

四、实践汉语。

Practice your Chinese.

Your friend falls in love with a Chinese girl, but he doesn't know how to express his feelings. See if you can help him.

实用一点通
Cultural Tips

Fall in love with a Chinese but find it difficult to reveal your love for him/her? Try some Chinese solutions then; and most of them are indirect ways. For example, you can give him/her a gift that you know he/she likes; instead of saying "I love you", choose packing paper with these words or patterns of hearts for the gift. Apart from a cleverly prepared gift, you can also do something sweet for him/her. For example, a boy can offer to escort the girl home or invite her out for a movie or concert, while a girl can do some chores for the boy. Your love will know your heart if you really care about him/her.

应变百宝囊
Language Enrichment

❶ 不错，我非常喜欢。

Búcuò, wǒ fēicháng xǐhuan.

Thanks, I like it very much.

❷ 真不愧是专家啊!

Zhēn búkuì shì zhuānjiā a!

You are really an expert.

❸ 你的建议太棒了!

Nǐ de jiànyì tài bàng le!

Your suggestion is great.

❹ 这样好极了!

Zhèyàng hǎojí le!

Great!

38 Lesson 38

祝愿

Zhùyuàn

Best Wishes

学习主题 Subject

There are different wishes for different festivals, situations or special days. Choose an appropriate one to suit your need.

学习重点 Language Focus

重点词 Key Words and Phrases

❶	一路	yílù	*n.*	all the way
❷	平安	píng'ān	*adj.*	safe and sound
❸	小心	xiǎoxīn	*adj.*	careful
❹	生日	shēngrì	*n.*	birthday
❺	快乐	kuàilè	*adj.*	happy
❻	恭喜	gōngxǐ	*v.*	congratulate
❼	同喜	tóngxǐ	*IE.*	thank you for your congratulations

重点句 Key Sentences

❶ 一路平安！
Yílù píng'ān
Have a safe trip!

❷ 生日快乐！
Shēngrì kuàilè!
Happy birthday!

❸ 恭喜，恭喜！
Gōngxǐ, gōngxǐ!
Congratulations!

❹ 同喜，同喜！
Tóngxǐ, tóngxǐ!
Thank you for your congratulations!

会话示例 Dialogues

I

[火车站。]

李力：汪洋，一路平安！路上小心。

汪洋：谢谢。

李力：到了桂林给我打电话吧。

汪洋：好的，好的，我走啦！

李力：再见！

汪洋：再见！

李力：一路平安啊！

[Huǒchēzhàn.]

Lǐ Lì: Wāng Yáng, yílù píng'ān! Lù shang xiǎoxīn.

Wāng Yáng: Xièxie.

Lǐ Lì: Dàole Guìlín gěi wǒ dǎ diànhuà ba.

Wāng Yáng: Hǎo de, hǎo de, wǒ zǒu la!

Lǐ Lì: Zàijiàn!

Wāng Yáng: Zàijiàn!

Lǐ Lì: Yílù píng'ān a!

II

嘉嘉：舅舅，生日快乐！

张明：谢谢，嘉嘉。

张妈：小明，生日快乐！今天妈妈①给你做好吃的，叫你的朋友一起来吧。

张明：好的，好的，谢谢妈。

Jiājia: Jiùjiu, shēngrì kuàilè!

Zhāng Míng: Xièxie, Jiājia.

Zhāng Mā: Xiǎo Míng, shēngrì kuàilè! Jīntiān māma gěi nǐ zuò hǎochī de, jiào nǐ de péngyou yìqǐ lái ba.

Zhāng Míng: Hǎo de, hǎo de, xièxie mā.

注释 Notes

I

[*At the railway station.*]

Li Li: Wang Yang, bon voyage! Take care!

Wang Yang: Thank you!

Li Li: Call me when you reach Guilin.

Wang Yang: OK. I've got to go.

Li Li: Bye!

Wang Yang: Bye!

Li Li: Have a safe journey!

II

Jiajia: Uncle, happy birthday!

Zhang Ming: Thank you, Jiajia!

Mother: Xiao Ming, happy birthday! I'll prepare some delicious dishes for you. Why not invite your friends to come over?

Zhang Ming: OK, thanks, Mom!

① Chinese often use words addressing relatives to address non-relatives in order to indicate closeness. Apart from that, people also tend to use the words with which kids address them to address themselves. For instance,

A：阿姨再见！

Āyí zàijiàn!

Bye, Aunty.

B：有时间来阿姨家玩儿！

Yǒu shíjiān lái āyí jiā wánr!

Come again to Aunty's home when you have time.

In addition, although Zhang Ming is no more a child, yet in the eyes of his mother, kids are always kids.

会话示例 Dialogues

Ⅲ

[王浩喜得贵子，亲戚朋友登门祝贺。]

王浩：姑姑来啦！

姑姑：恭喜②你啊，王浩！

王浩：同喜，同喜。姑夫请进！

姑夫：大哥、大嫂，恭喜你们啦！

王浩爸：同喜，同喜！

姑姑：我们进去看看孩子吧！

王浩爸：去，去看看。

[Wáng Hào xǐ dé guìzǐ, qīnqi péngyou dēng mén zhùhè.]

Wáng Hào: Gūgu lái la!

Gūgu: Gōngxǐ nǐ a, Wáng Hào!

Wáng Hào: Tóngxǐ, tóngxǐ. Gūfu qǐng jìn!

Gūfu: Dà gē、dà sǎo, gōngxǐ nǐmen la!

Wáng Hào bà: Tóngxǐ, tóngxǐ!

Gūgu: Wǒmen jìnqu kànkan háizi ba!

Wáng Hào bà: Qù , qù kànkan.

注释 Notes

III

[Wang Hao gets a baby boy. His relatives come to congratulate him.]

Wang Hao: Aunt, come on in!

Aunt: Congratulations, Wang Hao!

Wang Hao: Thank you! Uncle, come in!

Uncle: Brother, Sister, congratulations!

Wang Hao's father: Thanks!

Aunt: Let's go in and see the baby.

Wang Hao's father: OK!

② In China, when your friends are promoted, get married or have newly-born babies, you can say "恭喜" to offer your congratulations. You may also say "恭喜你" and add the reason of congratulations after that. Meanwhile you can fold your hands in front of your chest. Hearing your congratulations, your friends will say "同喜同喜" to thank you, hoping you are sharing their happiness as well.

练习
Exercises

一、在右栏给左栏的汉字找到相应的英文释义。
Match the Chinese expressions with the English ones.

平安	píng'ān	body
恭喜	gōngxǐ	health
身体	shēntǐ	careful
健康	jiànkāng	safe and sound
小心	xiǎoxīn	congratulations

二、根据英文提示，用汉语说出下面的句子。
Translate the following sentences into Chinese.

1. Have a safe trip!

____

2. Happy birthday to you!

____

3. Congratulations!

____

三、根据语境，完成对话。
Complete the dialogues according to the context.

1. A girl walks towards the departure gate, and a boy waves goodbye.

The girl: 我走了。
Wǒ zǒu le.
I've got to go!

The boy: ______________

2. A person greets a couple at their wedding.

A：我们结婚了。

Wǒmen jié hūn le.

We're married!

B：________________

3. A girl presents a lovely birthday cake to her friend.

A：啊！今天是我的生日，我都忘记了。

À! Jīntiān shì wǒ de shēngrì, wǒ dōu wàngjì le.

Oh, today's my birthday. I almost forget.

B：________________

四、实践汉语。

Practice your Chinese.

You are invited to a Chinese friend's wedding. Congratulate the couple.

实用一点通 Cultural Tips

Chinese will say different wishes for different festivals and special days. Find seasonal greeting cards at a bookstore, a stationery store or a florist when these days are coming and show your friendship and care for your friends.

应变百宝囊
Language Enrichment

❶ 祝你一切顺利！
Zhù nǐ yíqiè shùnlì!
Good luck!

❷ 祝你万事如意！
Zhù nǐ wànshì rúyì!
May everything be as you wish!

❸ 祝你生活愉快！
Zhù nǐ shēnghuó yúkuài!
Wishing you happiness everyday!

❹ 祝你全家幸福！
Zhù nǐ quánjiā xìngfú!
May your family be happy and blessed!

❺ 祝你岁岁平安！
Zhù nǐ suì suì píng'ān!
May every year be safe and peaceful!

❻ 祝你新年快乐！
Zhù nǐ xīnnián kuàilè!
Happy New Year!

❼ 恭喜你们喜结良缘！
Gōngxǐ nǐmen xǐ jié liángyuán!
Congratulations on your marriage!

❽ 祝你们白首偕老！
Zhù nǐmen báishǒu xié lǎo!
May you have a happy marriage!

⑨ 祝您健康长寿！
Zhù nín jiànkāng chángshòu!
Wishing you a long life with good health!

⑩ 愿您福如东海，寿比南山！
Yuàn nín fú rú dōnghǎi, shòu bǐ nánshān!
Wish you a long life and boundless happiness!

⑪ 祝你马到成功！
Zhù nǐ mǎ dào chénggōng!
Wishing you success!

⑫ 祝你事业有成！
Zhù nǐ shìyè yǒuchéng!
Wishing you success in your career!

⑬ 恭喜你喜得贵子！
Gōngxǐ nǐ xǐ dé guìzǐ!
Congratulations on the newly-born!

⑭ 恭喜你找到了理想的工作！
Gōngxǐ nǐ zhǎodàole lǐxiǎng de gōngzuò!
Congratulations on finding an ideal job!

参考答案
Keys to Exercises

Lesson 21

一、1.请多吃一点儿。
　　2.这菜很好吃。
三、1.吃好了，谢谢。
　　2.谢谢。

Lesson 22

一、你想喝（一）点儿什么？
　　我要一壶绿茶。
三、有　还有　要　来　壶
四、1.来一杯绿茶。
　　2.来一杯咖啡。
　　3.来一瓶可乐。

Lesson 23

一、1.现在几点？
　　2.我们八点十分见。
二、1.六点一刻。
　　2.九点半。
三、1.几点
　　2.什么
　　3.哪儿

Lesson 24

一、你什么时候开始不舒服？
　　我早上八点半上班。
三、1.你上午常常做什么？
　　2.星期六你常常做什么？
　　3.电影晚上七点十分开始。

Lesson 25

二、1.壶
　　2.杯　瓶
　　3.张
四、1.九月二号的　两张
　　2.有《神话》的票吗　五张

Lesson 26

三、1.我找小王。
　　2.喂。请问，小张在吗？
　　3.好，再见。

Lesson 27

三、1.D　2.C
四、1.哪儿有电话/电话在哪儿
　　2.请转2011

Lesson 28

二、1.他觉得有点儿头疼。
　　小张觉得有点儿冷。
　　我觉得有点儿不舒服。

2.老王头很疼。
　她肚子有点儿疼。
三、1.你怎么了？
2.我觉得有点儿冷。
3.可是觉得有点儿恶心。

Lesson 29

二、1.哪儿有医院？
2.这药怎么吃？
3.我要感冒药。
三、1.A　2.B　3.D　4.C

Lesson 30

二、1.您多大年纪了？
2.你肚子好了吗？
三、1.您多大年纪了？
2.你多大了？

Lesson 31

二、1.你是哪国人？
2.你做什么工作？

Lesson 32

二、1.今天不冷也不热，很舒服。
2.明天要下雾，开车小心点儿。
3.明天有雨，记着多穿点儿衣服。
三、1.怎么样　雾
2.不冷也不热
3.挺

Lesson 33

三、1.这是我的一点儿心意。
2.和你在一起我们很高兴。

Lesson 34

三、1.A　2.C　3.B

Lesson 35

三、1.A　2.B　3.F

Lesson 36

三、1.我累了　我有点儿渴
2.他怎么可以这样呢

Lesson 37

三、我喜欢你！
生日快乐！你今天真漂亮！
你的孩子真可爱！
太谢谢你了！

Lesson 38

二、1.一路平安！
2.生日快乐！
3.恭喜你！/恭喜恭喜！
三、1.路上小心。
2.恭喜你们！
3.生日快乐！

词语索引
Index of Words and Phrases

22	茶馆	cháguǎn	*n.*	tea house
26	查询	cháxún	*v.*	inquire
38	长寿	chángshòu	*n./adj.*	longevity; long life
25	成人票	chéngrénpiào	*np.*	adult ticket
22	橙汁	chéngzhī	*np.*	orange juice
29	冲剂	chōngjì	*n.*	instant herbal mixture
24	处理	chǔlǐ	*v.*	deal with
21	穿	chuān	*v.*	wear
25	船票	chuánpiào	*np.*	steamer ticket
23	次	cì	*m.*	train number
23	从	cóng	*prep.*	from
31	凑合	còuhe	*adj.*	not too bad
26	打	dǎ	*v.*	call
29	打针	dǎ zhēn	*v.*	give or take an in-jection
30	大	dà	*adj.*	old
32	大风	dà fēng	*n.*	gust
38	大哥	dàgē	*n.*	elder brother
38	大嫂	dàsǎo	*n.*	sister-in-law
35	打球	dǎ qiú	*vp.*	play ball
33	代	dài	*prep.*	on one's behalf
32	带	dài	*v.*	bring
36	担心	dān xīn	*v.*	be worried
35	但是	dànshì	*conj.*	but
33	蛋糕	dàngāo	*n.*	cake
36	倒霉	dǎo méi	*adj.*	have bad luck
23	地铁	dìtiě	*n.*	subway
23	点	diǎn	*n.*	o'clock
26	电话	diànhuà	*n.*	telephone
26	电话卡	diànhuàkǎ	*np.*	telephone card

24	电视	diànshì	*n.*	TV
25	电影票	diànyǐngpiào	*np.*	movie ticket
23	电影院	diànyǐngyuàn	*n.*	cinema; movie theatre
28	肚子	dùzi	*n.*	stomach
32	度	dù	*m.*	*unit or measurement for temperature*
33	对了	duì le	*IE.*	*used to arouse one's attention to sth.*
37	多	duō	*adv.*	to a great extent
30	多大	duō dà	*qp.*	how old
21	多谢	duō xiè	*IE.*	thanks a lot
32	多云	duōyún	*adj.*	cloudy
28	恶心	ěxin	*adj.*	feel like vomiting
25	儿童票	értóngpiào	*np.*	child ticket
32	而且	érqiě	*conj.*	and; but also
24	发烧	fā shāo	*v.*	have a fever
28	发炎	fāyán	*v.*	have inflammation
36	烦	fán	*adj.*	be tired of
23	飞机	fēijī	*n.*	airplane
23	飞机场	fēijīchǎng	*np.*	airport
25	(飞)机票	(fēi)jīpiào	*n.*	air ticket
23	分	fēn	*n.*	minute
26	分机	fēnjī	*n.*	extension (number)
32	风沙	fēngshā	*n.*	sand blown by wind
34	奉陪	fèngpéi	*v.*	accompany
38	福如东海	fú rú dōnghǎi	*IE.*	(expression of good wishes) happiness as boundless as the sea
21	付	fù	*v.*	pay
34	该……了	gāi……le	*IE.*	It's time…

35	改天	gǎitiān	*adv.*	sometime later; another day
21	干杯	gān bēi	*vp.*	drink a toast; bottoms up
32	干燥	gānzào	*adj.*	dry
28	感冒	gǎnmào	*v.*	have a cold
27	刚	gāng	*adv.*	just
31	高	gāo	*adj.*	tall; high
33	高档	gāodàng	*adj.*	top grade
29	膏药	gāoyào	*n.*	plaster
34	告辞	gàocí	*v.*	say goodbye to sb.
27	告(诉)	gào(su)	*v.*	tell
33	给	gěi	*v.*	give
37	更	gèng	*adv.*	more
31	工资	gōngzī	*n.*	wage
31	工作	gōngzuò	*n.*	job
23	公共汽车	gōnggòng qìchē	*n.*	bus
24	公司	gōngsī	*n.*	company
25	公用	gōngyòng	*adj.*	public
38	恭喜	gōngxǐ	*v.*	congratulate
38	姑夫	gūfu	*n.*	uncle; husband of father's sister
38	姑姑	gūgu	*n.*	aunt; father's sister
36	姑娘	gūniang	*n.*	young woman; girl
21	古老肉	Gǔlǎo Ròu	*pn.*	Sweet and sour pork
32	刮(风)	guā (fēng)	*v.*	(of the wind) blow
33	贵重	guìzhòng	*adj.*	expensive
25	桂林	Guìlín	*pn.*	Guilin
31	国	guó	*n.*	nation; country
26	国际长途	guójì chángtú	*np.*	IDD

26	国内长途	guónèi chángtú	*np.*	DDD
22	果汁	guǒzhī	*n.*	juice
31	过得去	guò de qù	*IE.*	passable; not hard
23	过街天桥	guòjiē tiānqiáo	*np.*	overpass
35	过两天	guò liǎng tiān	*IE.*	after a couple of days
28	过敏	guòmǐn	*v.*	be allergic
22	还是	háishi	*conj.*	or
30	孩子	háizi	*n.*	child
31	海淀图书大厦	Hǎidiàn Túshū Dàshà	*pn.*	Haidian Book Building
29	含片	hánpiàn	*n.*	lozenge
30	好	hǎo	*adj.*	well
37	好	hǎo	*adv.*	very; quite
21	好吃	hǎochī	*adj.*	delicious
21	好的	hǎo de	*IE.*	OK; all right
35	好好儿	hǎohāor	*adv.*	to one's heart's content
21	好看	hǎokàn	*adj.*	good-looking; look nice
25	号	hào	*n.*	date
22	喝	hē	*v.*	drink
33	盒子	hézi	*n.*	box
33	红包	hóngbāo	*n.*	red envelope containing money
22	红茶	hóngchá	*n.*	black tea
22	红酒	hóngjiǔ	*n.*	red wine
26	后	hòu	*n.*	after
22	壶	hú	*n.*	pot
37	花	huā	*n.*	flower
22	花茶	huāchá	*n.*	scented tea
26	话费	huàfèi	*n.*	telephone rate; charge
31	黄色	huángsè	*n.*	yellow

26	回	huí	*v.*	reply to (a phone call)
21	回锅肉	Huíguō Ròu	*pn.*	Twice cooked pork
29	回家	huí jiā	*vp.*	go home
32	会	huì	*part.*	shall
23	火车	huǒchē	*n.*	train
25	火车票	huǒchēpiào	*np.*	train ticket
23	火车站	huǒchēzhàn	*np.*	railway station
24	或者	huòzhě	*conj.*	or
37	……极了	……jí le	*adv.*	extremely
23	几	jǐ	*qp.*	how many
32	记	jì	*v.*	remember
24	家	jiā	*n.*	home
31	加拿大	Jiānádà	*pn.*	Canada
23	见面	jiàn miàn	*v.*	meet
38	健康	jiànkāng	*adj.*	healthy
32	降温	jiàng wēn	*v.*	a drop of temperature
29	胶囊	jiāonáng	*n.*	capsule
31	叫	jiào	*v.*	be called
38	叫	jiào	*v.*	invite
27	接	jiē	*v.*	receive
24	接待	jiēdài	*v.*	receive
30	结婚	jié hūn	*v.*	marry
24	今天	jīntiān	*n.*	today
38	进去	jìnqu	*v.*	go into
21	京酱肉丝	Jīngjiàng Ròusī	*pn.*	Sweet shredded pork with Chinese onions
25	经济舱	jīngjìcāng	*np.*	economy class
27	酒店	jiǔdiàn	*n.*	hotel
26	就这样吧	jiù zhèyàng ba	*IE.*	be it so
38	舅舅	jiùjiu	*n.*	uncle; mother's brother

28	觉得	juéde	*v.*	feel
22	咖啡	kāfēi	*n.*	coffee
32	开车	kāi chē	*v.*	drive
37	开(花)	kāi (huā)	*v.*	blossom
24	开会	kāi huì	*v.*	have a meeting
24	开始	kāishǐ	*v.*	begin; start
28	看病	kàn bìng	*v.*	see a doctor
35	考虑	kǎolǜ	*v.*	think over;consider
28	咳嗽	késou	*v.*	cough
22	可乐	kělè	*n.*	coke
28	可能	kěnéng	*adv.*	maybe
36	渴	kě	*adj.*	thirsty
23	刻	kè	*n.*	quarter
24	客户	kèhù	*n.*	client
33	客气	Kèqi	*adj.*	polite
21	口水鸡	Kǒushuǐ Jī	*pn.*	Spicy Sichuan chicken
38	快乐	kuàilè	*adj.*	happy
22	矿泉水	kuàngquánshuǐ	*n.*	mineral water
36	困	kùn	*adj.*	drowsy
28	拉肚子	lā dùzi	*vp.*	have diarrhoea
21	辣子鸡丁	Làzi Jīdīng	*pn.*	Diced chicken with chili
36	啦	la	*mdpt.*	*to express exdamation and interrogation*
31	蓝色	lánsè	*n.*	blue
31	老外	lǎowài	*n.*	foreigner
36	累	lèi	*adj.*	be tired
28	冷	lěng	*adj.*	cold
33	礼物	lǐwù	*n.*	gift; present
38	理想	lǐxiǎng	*n.*	ideal

25	联票	liánpiào	*n.*	coupon ticket
24	联系	liánxì	*v.*	contact
37	亮	liàng	*adj.*	bright
23	列车	lièchē	*n.*	train
23	零	líng	*num.*	zero
26	留言	liú yán	*v.*	leave a message
28	流鼻涕	liú bítì	*vp.*	have a runny nose
29	流血	liú xiě	*v.*	bleed
23	轮船	lúnchuán	*n.*	ship
26	吕	Lǚ	*pn.*	a surname
33	旅游	lǚyóu	*v./n.*	travel
22	绿茶	lǜchá	*n.*	green tea
38	妈(妈)	mā (ma)	*n.*	mother
34	麻烦	máfan	*v.*	bother
36	麻烦	máfan	*adj.*	troublesome
21	麻婆豆腐	Mápó Dòufu	*pn.*	Bean curd cooked in hot sauce
38	马到成功	mǎ dào chénggōng	*IE.*	win instant success
23	码头	mǎtou	*n.*	dock
25	买	mǎi	*v.*	buy
25	卖	mài	*v.*	sell
33	满意	mǎnyì	*adj.*	be satisfied
34	忙	máng	*adj.*	busy
34	没什么	méi shénme	*IE.*	it doesn't matter
27	没(有)	méi (yǒu)	*v.*	have not; not yet
31	美国	Měiguó	*pn.*	the United States
23	门口	ménkǒu	*n.*	doorway
25	门票	ménpiào	*n.*	admission ticket
24	秘书	mìshū	*n.*	secretary
26	免费	miǎnfèi	*v.*	free of charge

25	免票	miǎnpiào	*v./n.*	free of charge
31	名字	míngzi	*n.*	name
37	那边	nàbiān	*pron.*	there
35	难	nán	*adj.*	hard; difficult
35	能	néng	*v.*	can; be able to
30	年纪	niánjì	*n.*	age
22	牛奶	niúnǎi	*n.*	milk
31	欧洲	Ōuzhōu	*pn.*	Europe
28	呕吐	ǒutù	*v.*	vomit
32	爬	pá	*v.*	climb
31	胖	pàng	*adj.*	(of human body) fat
33	陪	péi	*v.*	accompany
38	朋友	péngyou	*n.*	friend
36	碰	pèng	*v.*	touch
22	啤酒	píjiǔ	*n.*	beer
25	票	piào	*n.*	ticket
37	漂亮	piàoliang	*adj.*	beautiful
30	拼	pīn	*v.*	spell
38	平安	píng'ān	*adj.*	safe and sound
24	起床	qǐ chuáng	*v.*	get up
30	起来(看起来)	qǐlai (kàn qǐlai)	*v.*	*used after a verb to indicate estimation*
23	汽车站	qìchēzhàn	*np.*	bus stop
22	汽水	qìshuǐ	*n.*	soda
26	乔	Qiáo	*pn.*	a surname
35	巧	qiǎo	*adj.*	coincidental
32	晴	qíng	*adj.*	fine; clear
32	晴转阴	qíng zhuǎn yīn	*vp.*	sunny to overcast
35	球	qiú	*n.*	ball
26	区号	qūhào	*n.*	area code
38	全家	quánjiā	*n.*	whole family

32	热	rè	*adj.*	hot
27	人	rén	*n.*	person; people
31	日子	rìzi	*n.*	life
25	软卧	ruǎnwò	*n.*	soft sleeper
32	伞	sǎn	*n.*	umbrella
28	嗓子	sǎngzi	*n.*	throat
32	山	shān	*n.*	mountain
24	上班	shàng bān	*v.*	go to work
23	上海	Shànghǎi	*pn.*	Shanghai
32	上课	shàng kè	*v.*	attend class
24	上午	shàngwǔ	*n.*	morning
26	谁	shéi/shuí	*qp.*	who; whom
30	身体	shēntǐ	*n.*	(human) body
24	什么	shénme	*qp.*	what
24	什么时候	shénme shíhou	*IE.*	when
25	神话	Shénhuà	*pn.*	Myth (a movie)
36	生病	shēng bìng	*vp.*	fall ill
38	生活	shēnghuó	*n.*	life
36	生气	shēng qì	*adj.*	angry
38	生日	shēngrì	*n.*	birthday
28	失眠	shī mián	*v.*	have insomnia
34	失陪	shīpéi	*v.*	unable to accompany sb.
32	湿润	shīrùn	*adj.*	wet
24	时候	shíhou	*n.*	(a point in) time
26	市内电话	shìnèi diànhuà	*np.*	local call
35	事(情)	shì(qing)	*n.*	thing
38	事业有成	shìyè yǒuchéng	*IE.*	make accomplishment in one's career
33	饰品	shìpǐn	*n.*	accessory
33	首饰	shǒushì	*n.*	jewelry

38	寿比南山	shòu bǐ nánshān	*IE.*	(expression of good wishes) a life as enduring as the Southern Mountain
24	舒服	shūfu	*adj.*	comfortable
22	水	shuǐ	*n.*	water
24	睡觉	shuì jiào	*v.*	sleep
38	顺利	shùnlì	*adj.*	smooth
36	司机	sījī	*n.*	driver
36	死	sǐ	*adj.*	dead
30	岁	suì	*m.*	age
26	她	tā	*pron.*	she
32	台风	táifēng	*n.*	typhoon
33	太	tài	*adv.*	too
37	特别	tèbié	*adv.*	especially
28	疼	téng	*adj.*	ache
29	体温	tǐwēn	*n.*	body temperature
25	天	tiān	*n.*	day
25	天津	Tiānjīn	*pn.*	Tianjin
32	天气	tiānqì	*n.*	weather
22	铁观音	Tiěguānyīn	*pn.*	Tieguanyin (tea)
32	挺	tǐng	*adv.*	very
38	同喜	tóngxǐ	*v.*	thank you for your congratulations
28	头	tóu	*n.*	head
25	头等舱	tóuděngcāng	*np.*	first class
31	头发	tóufa	*n.*	hair
28	头晕	tóuyūn	*v.*	dizzy
31	图书	túshū	*n.*	books
25	团体票	tuántǐpiào	*np.*	group ticket
21	完	wán	*v.*	finish
33	玩具	wánjù	*n.*	toy

24	晚饭	wǎnfàn	*n.*	supper; dinner
23	晚上	wǎnshang	*n.*	evening
38	万事如意	wànshì rúyì	*IE.*	may everything be as you wish
25	往返票	wǎngfǎnpiào	*np.*	return ticket
38	忘记	wàngjì	*v.*	forget
22	味道	wèidào	*n.*	taste
28	胃口	wèikǒu	*n.*	appetite
29	胃疼	wèi téng	*np.*	stomachache
26	喂	wèi	*int.*	hello
24	文件	wénjiàn	*n.*	file
21	闻	wén	*v.*	smell
31	问	wèn	*v.*	ask
22	乌龙茶	wūlóngchá	*n.*	oolong tea
24	午饭	wǔfàn	*n.*	lunch
32	雾	wù	*n.*	fog
38	喜得贵子	xǐ dé guìzǐ	*IE.*	congratulate on the newborn
37	喜欢	xǐhuan	*v.*	like
38	喜结良缘	xǐ jié liángyuán	*IE.*	congratulate on one's marriage
32	下	xià	*v.*	(of rain, snow, etc.) fall
24	下班	xià bān	*v.*	be off duty
24	下课	xià kè	*v.*	finish class
24	下午	xiàwǔ	*n.*	afternoon
35	下(一)次	xià (yí) cì	*n.*	next time
34	先	xiān	*adv.*	earlier
33	鲜花	xiānhuā	*n.*	flower
27	香江酒店	Xiāngjiāng Jiǔdiàn	*pn.*	Xiangjiang Hotel
28	消化不良	xiāohuà bùliáng	*np.*	indigestion
29	消炎	xiāo yán	*v.*	diminish inflammation

32	小到中雨	xiǎo dào zhōng yǔ	*vp.*	light to moderate rain
38	小心	xiǎoxīn	*adj.*	careful
30	写	xiě	*v.*	write
34	辛苦	xīnkǔ	*v.*	toil
38	新年	xīnnián	*n.*	new year
33	心意	xīnyì	*n.*	regards, kind feeling
29	行	xíng	*v.*	OK
38	幸福	xìngfú	*adj.*	happy
30	休假	xiū jià	*v.*	take a holiday
34	休息	xiūxi	*v.*	have a rest
32	雪	xuě	*n.*	snow
29	血压	xuèyā	*n.*	blood pressure
35	研究	yánjiū	*v.*	research
37	眼睛	yǎnjing	*n.*	eye
29	药	yào	*n.*	medicine
29	药店	yàodiàn	*n.*	drugstore; pharmacy
29	药丸	yàowán	*n.*	pill
25	野蛮师姐	Yěmán Shījiě	*pn.*	Windstruck (a movie)
29	医院	yīyuàn	*n.*	hospital
27	一定	yídìng	*adv.*	must; certainly
34	一会儿	yíhuìr	*n.*	for a moment
38	一路	yílù	*n.*	all the way
38	一路平安	yílù píng'ān	*IE.*	have a safe tirp
38	一切	yíqiè	*pron.*	all
32	一样	yíyàng	*adj.*	same
21	（一）点儿	(yì) diǎnr	*m.*	a little; a bit
35	已经	yǐjīng	*adv.*	already
32	阴	yīn	*adj.*	overcast
24	音乐	yīnyuè	*n.*	music
31	英国	Yīngguó	*pn.*	U.K.; the Great Britain

25	硬卧	yìngwò	*n.*	hard sleeper
25	硬座	yìngzuò	*n.*	hard seat
28	哟	yō	*mdpt.*	*expressing surprise*
33	游览	yóulǎn	*v.*	visit
35	有（一）点儿	yǒu (yì) diǎnr	*adv.*	a little; a bit
38	愉快	yúkuài	*adj.*	happy
32	雨	yǔ	*n.*	rain
32	雨夹雪	yǔ jiā xuě	*vp.*	sleet; rain mixed with snow
36	郁闷	yùmèn	*adj.*	gloomy
24	预约	yùyuē	*v.*	make a reservation/ an appointment
34	远送	yuǎn sòng	*vp.*	see a visitor off far
38	愿	yuàn	*v.*	wish
35	约会	yuēhuì	*n.*	appointment
25	月	yuè	*n.*	month
26	在	zài	*v.*	be at; be in
36	脏	zāng	*adj.*	dirty
34	早	zǎo	*adj.*	early
24	早上	zǎoshang	*n.*	morning
28	怎么	zěnme	*qp.*	how; why
36	怎么办	zěnme bàn	*vp.*	what to do
25	张	zhāng	*m.*	*for paper, desk, etc.*
36	长大	zhǎngdà	*vp.*	grow up
36	着急	zháo jí	*adj.*	anxious
26	找	zhǎo	*v.*	look for
26	这样	zhèyàng	*pron.*	such
37	真	zhēn	*adv.*	really
37	真的	zhēn de	*IE.*	true
25	正好	zhènghǎo	*adv.*	just right
27	……中	……zhōng	*prep.*	in the middle of
31	中国	Zhōngguó	*pn.*	China

24	中午	zhōngwǔ	*n.*	noon
38	祝	zhù	*v.*	wish
27	转	zhuǎn	*v.*	transfer
27	转接	zhuǎnjiē	*v.*	transfer
26	总机	zǒngjī	*n.*	switchboard (number)
34	走	zǒu	*v.*	leave
32	最低气温	zuì dī qìwēn	*np.*	the lowest temperature
32	最高气温	zuì gāo qìwēn	*np.*	the highest temperature